You'll be sorry when I'm dead

Marieke Hardy

ALLEN&UNWIN

First published in 2011

Allen & Unwin
Sydney, Melbourne, Auckland, London

83 Alexander Street
Crows Nest NSW 2065
Australia
Phone: (61 2) 8425 0100
Fax: (61 2) 9906 2218
Email: info@allenandunwin.com
Web: www.allenandunwin.com

Cataloguing-in-Publication details are available
from the National Library of Australia
www.trove.nla.gov.au

ISBN 978 1 74237 726 1

Set in 13/16 pt Bembo by Post Pre-press Group, Australia

10 9 8 7 6 5 4 3 2 1

For Gabi

Contents

A foreword by my father

Marieke Hardy is my daughter. If you are reading this, it means her new book has been published.

As the writer of this book she has used the real names of people she writes about.

I argued long and loud with her that it is 'better', or rather 'safer', to fictionalise names and events in one's writing to avoid hurting the real people—and indeed the writer!

Then I have to remember that her grandfather used a fake name of a real person and even changed what happened to them yet still got into a mess of trouble.

Her grandfather, my father, Prank Hartley (not his real name) wrote a novel entitled *Powder without Chlorine* (not its real name). In this novel he followed the life of a fictional character who was based on a real person, Ron Rebb (not his real name). In the book the writer had the fictional character do things that the 'real' character did not do.

Was it legitimate fiction or was it an attack on a real person?

The court found for the writer. It was a work of fiction. The argument lives on.

My father also wrote himself into another book as FJ Borky (not his real name), a struggling left-wing writer hiding from debt collectors. This was alarmingly close to the truth.

It must be clear to all but the most obtuse among you that real versus fictional names can be a nightmare not only for those written about but for the writer whose relationships can be put under real strain.

I admire the talent of my daughter and love her writing. It is truthful, emotionally honest and revealing of the human condition. Yet could she not achieve the same ends without the real names?

But she is a wonderful writer for all that and I will read this book when it is delivered to me where I currently reside.

Alwyn Hadley (not my real name)
Somewhere on a beach near Bridgetown, Barbados
(I no longer appear in public.)

You can lead a horticulture

At the age of eleven I decided with no small sense of certainty that when I grew up I wanted to become a prostitute. I was so convinced by this as a path of righteousness I felt comfortable enough announcing my intentions to not only my close circle of girlfriends, but also the elderly Vietnamese couple who ran the local milk bar. I can't recall their exact reaction at the time, but they were usually very supportive of my scamp-like antics and, besides, their English wasn't the best so they very likely nodded and smiled and gave me a free Wizz Fizz, which seemed to be their go-to response with the more wayward neighbourhood children.

For some reason my parents weren't as excited about the idea. Attempts were made to talk me around, but I was a child of strong will.

'Mum . . . Dad . . . I appreciate your concerns,' I told them one night over a traditional Friday fish-finger dinner, 'but this is just how it is. Being a prostitute is my dream. I wish you'd understand that and show some support.'

Musical theatre is entirely to blame for this sudden and arresting career decision. Musical theatre, combined with those first illicit throes of nocturnal explorations beneath an embroidered doona; awkward, arching contortions in flannelette pyjama pants. I dreamt of A-ha's Morten Harket and his 'confusing' leather bracelets, possibly setting the scene for a future interest in BDSM.

The sum of masturbation and musical theatre was almost crippling in my case—it seemed I leapt overnight from cheerily faking Xavier Roberts' autograph on the buttocks of cut-price Cabbage Patch Kids to plotting an illustrious career as an underage streetwalker. Performances of *Godspell* and *Jesus Christ Superstar* should be forward announced with a grim warning for young ladies: abandon hope all ye who enter here. Musicals are sticky and dangerous, and they lead by tempting example. The seamier characters in the cast always get the best songs, the rudest, most inviting dance numbers, the most enticingly risqué costumes. Productions like *Sweet Charity* and *Cabaret*, where rows and rows of intensely beautiful, saucy whores, decked out in hotpants and fishnet stockings and bowler hats, high-kick their way around wooden chairs—which seems, in hindsight, a misguidedly cheery response to their presumably bleak working conditions—inevitably make prostitution appear an exciting profession. If selling one's soul to the devil involved face makeup and a sequinned bow tie, as a child I was mystified as to why parlour madams weren't beating off potential employees with a stick. Perhaps if veterinary nurses were allowed to wear feather boas and false eyelashes I may have been equally enamoured with the idea of sticking my hand inside dogs' vaginas.

As a pre-pubescent, masturbation was a revelation; a ticket out of dullsville directly into the sticky, pulsating, heady area of grownups. Somewhere along this naïve and playful voyage of physical discovery I decided that if touching oneself in the lap area felt so good it was only natural that prostitutes—who were touched on their laps a great deal, if schoolyard rumours were to be believed—felt good all day long. Combined with the glamour of musical theatre, it was a no-brainer.

Suffice to say I never quite achieved the dream—despite what you may read in the Murdoch press—and as an adult I ceased aspiring to be a prostitute and instead became fixated on whether my boyfriends had slept with one. I pushed and prodded my long-suffering partners; bullied them in those easy, unguarded moments that creep in during lengthy afternoons touching toes beneath beer garden tables. I wanted to know obscene details and lurid insights, to get the inside story on what exactly happened when you were alone in a room with someone you'd just *paid for sex*. Who made the first move? What would be your opening gambit? Did anyone fumble with a bra? Was there even a bra?

'You can tell *me*,' I would say with a general air of what I hoped was cheer and trustworthiness. 'I'm not *worried*. I'm not going to *judge* you.' Whether the men involved had been burnt by such breezy assurances by girlfriends in the past, or had lived a life remarkably sin free, they were nonetheless too smart to buy into my games and left me anecdote-poor and hungry for knowledge. I still wanted to understand what went on behind the velvet curtain, or smeared sliding door or, in the case of some less salubrious outer suburban businesses, bullet-riddled flyscreen. Red lights and buzzing fluorescents and lamps with shawls draped over them, value packs of lubricants, massage oil that smelt like cupboards. My assumptions about the world of prostitution were cartoonish at best.

Certainly strip clubs had always been accessible, but I'd never seen the point of them. All that money being thrown around in sticky wads, just so a frightened-looking meter maid might indelicately shove her gusset in your face. There was no touching the talent, and if a chap got even the slightest semblance of a hard-on he was tapped on the shoulder and politely asked to leave. Why bother? The thought of all those men standing around in meaty clumps, sniggering and snorting and gaping open-mouthed, not knowing where to put their fingers or their beers, then climbing into their cars with straining erections and heading home for a sad diddle in the shower seemed simply ludicrous.

The last time I'd been to Melbourne strip club Spearmint Rhino my friend Gen had drunk the bar clean of tequila and spent a disturbing amount of time in a dark corner making out with a stranger who was the spitting image of Shane Warne.

'I don't have my glasses on. Is he hot? Should I go home with him?' she slurred to the rest of us during a break from frantic necking. She was wearing a peaked cap with the words BEER SLUTZ emblazoned across the front.

'Gen. *No.*'

Gen winked and nodded at the same time, an action we would have thought physically impossible given the fact she'd just spent the last five minutes trying to eat a discarded peanut off the floor, and lurched off back in the direction of Warney and his unimpressed pals. We lost her for a little while after that, and became swept up in the typical social awkwardness that abounds when a group of inner-city wankers visit a strip club 'ironically'. We swung between snidely making fun of the stripper outfits, or acting as private ventriloquists and giving the dancers comedy voices ('Where did I put my Kilometrico? I fancy doing the cryptic once I'm offstage. Oh look, it's up here' etc.) and then lapsing into long, strained silences the moment something undeniably erotic occurred.

We were reminded of Gen's presence about forty minutes later when we saw her wedged smudgily between a pair of grim-faced bouncers who were in the process of frog-marching her to the exit. Obviously we rushed to defend her honour, something we perhaps should have done about three hours before when she'd made her first louche approach to the Spin King.

'What the hell's going on?'

The bouncers looked at us disparagingly.

'You with her?'

Gen smiled at us. She looked fairly cheery for somebody in the vice-like grip of two Samoan security guards, though this might have had something to do with the twelve tequila shots.

'Er . . . yeah.'

A nod from Bouncer A.

'Right. You're out too.'

Thus, en masse, we were turfed out of Spearmint Rhino ('Don't you know who I am? I was once a guest on *The Early Bird Show!*') and on to King Street. The shame of it.

'Even Gene Simmons doesn't get thrown out of strip joints,' my friend Dave the Scot said ruefully, watching the bouncers head back inside with an exchange of satisfied grunts. 'And I heard he sometimes goes to the toilet on the ladies' faces.'

Gen was grinning blurrily up at us from the gutter and could offer no explanation as to why she'd been so unceremoniously evicted, so we were forced to guess among ourselves what dreadful deed she might have committed. I mean, people jerk off in the men's room in those places. People vomit in pot plants. It's not like we were in *church*.

We eventually ended up at Wally's Bar in Collingwood, where my best friend Gabi stumbled upon a member from Jet wedged in the toilets between the cistern and the wall ('I think I'm stuck,' he told her in bewildered tones) and I drank one too many mojitos and fell across the dancefloor like Peter Garrett having an epileptic fit, much to the amusement of onlookers. It was a degrading evening for all concerned. And as far as I know, the young man from Jet is still trapped in the toilets.

No, strip clubs were for chumps and amateurs, schoolies and sailors on shore leave. And too pedestrian-accessible to hold any sense of allure, any opium-den, *Miss Saigon*-style titillation. I temporarily made do with strip clubs like an impatient gastronome shovelling through the entrée. Strip clubs were the support band. Prostitutes were the main act.

The problem is, as a novice it's impossible to know how to go about involving oneself in the world of prostitutes. There's no training manual, no checklist of Things To Do. It's easy enough to get drunk and flip through the Yellow Pages where almost everyone looks like the sort of terrifying Russian mail-order bride who would eat all your Vita Brits before ripping your throat out with her teeth, but making the phone call without collapsing into a fit of mortified giggles is another matter altogether. I still can't explain why I was so obsessively keen to experience a real life face-to-face encounter with a hooker. I'd like to say I'll try anything once, with the exception of voting conservative, but to be honest I'd almost definitely draw an additional line at putting Sugar Ray on a mix tape and having sex with a horse. Outside of that, I'm very open-minded, which is why when in my early twenties I finally chanced upon a ragingly libidinous gentleman caller with background experience in whores I was pretty well primed to get the unedited story.

Matty was what you would call 'wild at heart', if you were eighty years old and also prone to using expressions like 'dagnabbit' and 'there's a storm in these here achin' bones'. He was troubled, and he was Trouble. I had just ended a long-term cohabitation and felt endlessly reckless. I met him for the first time in the gardens next to the Exhibition Buildings in Carlton. It was dark and he said 'hello' and we just started kissing. I wanted to be around him all the time. He provided that addictive sense of freefall you get when you read Bukowski and start drinking whisky at 9 am, and the more I disentangled myself from my sad, worn-out old relationship and my tedious job writing commercial television, the more susceptible I was to his hazardous charms.

He would tell me stories of his stepfather, a dark and shady character who entertained gangster friends and occasionally carried a gun. Coming from the leafy streets of East Hawthorn where the most exciting thing to happen in twenty years was my dad once forgetting to wear pants whilst taking the garbage out (19/11/1982—you probably saw it on the news), this seemed hugely exotic. Matty had grown up in a world of drunken rages and cigarettes and bar-room brawls and drive-by shootings. He ran away from home in a whirl of self-righteousness and marijuana smoke. His stepfather beat his mother. Matty was of course brutally and emotionally damaged as a result. I found him intoxicating.

Finally, here was somebody who could not only shed some light on the elusive topic of brothels but also elaborate upon it with street smarts far beyond my comparatively sheltered capacity. As I listened with a combination of horror and awe he told me about the time he'd accidentally stumbled across his stepfather's illegal porno dubbing operation. ('Two VCRs linked to each other via a series of electrical leads,' he explained patiently. 'That's how they did it in those days.') He'd also figured out—after days of painstaking practice—how to break into his stepfather's safe. There he found ten thousand dollars in hundred-dollar bills. He immediately started pilfering from the pile. A little on a taxi ride here, a little more on a bottle of Beam there. One of the first major purchases he made with his illicit newfound wealth was a half-hour visit from an escort. He had dialled the number of the agency with trembling, I've-gone-too-far-to-stop-now fingers. Within the hour a prostitute had come around to his house and obediently sucked him off. He spent the rest of the evening celebrating in his room, getting blind drunk on red wine stolen from the downstairs liquor cabinet.

He was twelve years old.

This was my sort of chap.

During the course of his relatively young life Matty had fucked strippers, teenage runaways, good girls from the suburbs, rough girls from the coast, arty Fitzroy types with tattoos and open windows, motherly hippies smothered in avocado oil and sanctimony, and lots and lots of prostitutes. Rather than allow this fact to send me screaming in the other direction ('So you're really into whores? That's such an amazing coincidence, I love tapas bars and Spanish architecture'), I found it completely compelling. I had found my in-road.

We took on my secret obsession with gusto, tackling obstacles like a cheerily perverted street team. Once, during a fairly slow day at work, I requested that he go to a brothel and receive a blowjob while I listened on the telephone. People were swinging in and out of my office with script amendments and friendly 'I'll come back later when you're not so busy' mimes while I sat, absolutely transfixed, listening to my boyfriend apparently thoroughly enjoying himself with another woman. It felt fucked up and intense.

As an ominous sign of things to come Matty's phone ran out of credit and cut off partway through a fairly interesting moment where the young lady in question (young? middle-aged? hunchbacked? It was so hard to tell on the phone) had asked him if he *liked it*.

'Y—' Matty had purred, before the phone beeped angrily and he abruptly disappeared into the ether.

'If we're going to *do weird stuff like this*,' I wailed to him later in the night as we debriefed, '*you need to pay your phone bill*.'

The experience didn't deter us, miraculously. It made us bolder. We talked about trying out other, more provocative encounters and one night Matty authoritatively took what he felt to be the natural next step and called an escort over to my house.

I don't know how it happened. Yes I do. A drunkenly intimate conversation about his extensive experiences, no doubt with me once again cajoling him into revealing further details about his dalliances with winsome strip-a-grams ('Was she pretty? Did her underpants have Velcro fasteners?') had led to a series of teasing hypotheticals which in turn led to some kind of 'I dare you'/'No, I dare *you*' idiocy and all of a sudden, there you have it—we were standing in our kitchen wearing pyjamas and daunted expressions, and a lady of the night was on her way over.

My first thought at the time—for some reason—involved my dog, who I assumed should be morally protected from the forthcoming experience.

'We need to lock Bob Ellis in the laundry,' I said.

Matty seemed nonplussed.

'Why? She's been in the room before. During.'

'With *us*. This woman is a prostitute. I don't want her touching my dog. Or having some sort of . . . visitor relationship with her.'

The thought of some strumpet making coo-coo noises over Bob Ellis and scratching her behind the ear, being a normal dog person, was somehow just too much to bear. Put my boyfriend's dick in your mouth, fine. Tickle my dog's belly, get the hell out of my house. My dog didn't ask to be involved in any depraved sexual fantasies; she was simply a normal hound who liked chasing tennis balls. Having her sniffing about, wagging her sweet little tail, even—god forbid—barking high spiritedly to join in the orgiastic fun, somehow took the edge off the wickedness of it all. It was bad enough having my gym clothes and a library bag in the corner of my room. When did you ever see movies where a winking prostitute entertained a customer with a sports bra and a 'Ready, Steady, READ!!' tote bag within arm's reach?

I suddenly saw my house through a prostitute's eyes—or at least my clumsy assumptions of what a prostitute was, after all of Matty's *My Fair Lady*-esque teachings. I realised I now hated my 1950s salt and pepper shakers. I realised I now hated the fact I was too much of a teenage dolt to wash and put away my clothes. Why wouldn't I wash and put away my clothes? Other people washed and put away their clothes.

Most of all I hated that a stranger was going to be there passing judgement on my stuff and I would have to pay her for her time.

I panicked.

'What should a room look like when a prostitute comes over for a threeway?'

'I don't know. A room.'

'Maybe I should tidy up.'

'She's not Mary Poppins. She's not going to run a white glove over the furniture and then fly off with her umbrella.'

The closer it all got to becoming real, the more I felt I wasn't cut out for these kinds of scenarios. I'm all talk. I embrace the giddy, monstrously creative idea of something or someone over the actuality of its existence. I loved imagining the wickedly wry double entendres I would make to the Monica Bellucci lookalike once she arrived and the no-doubt intellectually engaging discourse that would serve as precursor to any sex act. In my head it was all wild and perfect and everyone involved was very good-looking and possessed of a keen sense of comic timing. Matty would wear a top hat and a spinning bow tie. My underwear would come off seamlessly without any awkward tugging or wriggling. It would be perfect. Yet in reality I was terrified, and experiencing what they no doubt knowingly refer to in escort circles as 'buyer's remorse'. I paced and wondered what on earth had brought us to this desperately sad and careless point. The moment the knock on the door came I disappeared to my bedroom like a coward and left Matty—the pro, the dirty, over-experienced, stripper-fucking pro—to deal with the pleasantries.

Our lady caller announced herself with all the delicacy and grace of Anna Nicole Smith on Oaks Day. 'GROUSE PLACE! HOW LONG HAVE YAS LIVED HERE?'

Her greeting echoed around the entrance hall. I looked around my room for somewhere to hide. I couldn't possibly face this. I'd written for *Neighbours*, for christ's sake. I had a blog. *I had gone to the same school as Peter Costello.*

Matty replied, 'Actually, I don't live here. My girlfriend does.'

'AW. WHERE'S SHE TONYTE?'

His response was brief, but honest. 'She's . . . hiding in the bedroom.'

I wanted him to die in a freak accident. A painful one that involved fire and a pair of pinking shears.

'WHYNTCHA GET HER THEN?'

Matty entered the bedroom with apologetic shrugs. I hissed at him, mimed furiously that this was a bad idea and I had made a dreadful mistake and if he could please ask her to leave and take an apricot cookie for her troubles on the way out I would be forever grateful. Instead, I was dragged from my hiding place and shoved into view like the youngest child of the Von Trapp Family Singers facing a pre-dinner performance.

I waved. I still can't believe I waved. Who *waves* at a *prostitute*?

'Hello there.'

She was roughly twenty-five years of age, she was roughly five foot four, and she was rough. Not in an obscene way, more like if you saw her at the Brownlow on the arm of Cameron Ling you'd think, 'Gosh, isn't it nice that Lingy's found someone to chat to?' She had long red hair and a tight khaki Supre skirt and she was beaming at us like we were her children and we'd just presented her with a Paddle-Pop-stick photo frame with the phrase WORLD'S TOPPEST MUM painted on it.

I really had no issue with her physically—she was kind of sweet, if you had consumed seven glasses of pinot gris and smudged your vision slightly—but I definitely wished she'd stop clasping her hands and saying 'LOOK AT YOUSE TWO!! SOOOOOO CUTE!!' every five minutes. In hindsight she was probably nervous and attempting to break the ice, but at the time I thought she was about thirty seconds away from spitting on a hanky and wiping dirt off my face with it.

I kept stealing helpless glances at Matty, who seemed happily ensconced in his role as host and instantly began leading our guest on a tour of the kitchen. Surely this was the moment a vaguely amusing idea became too real and everyone made polite noises about needing to go home and pay the sitter. It hardly seemed the time to leap into a life experience in which I was no longer certain I wanted to partake.

I'm not even sure what I wanted out of the whole deal anymore, outside of a rather ribald story to terrify my cousins with around the table on Christmas Day and a satisfied long-held curiosity about what a real-life prostitute would look like when not being depicted by the cast of Foxtel's successful Australian drama series *Satisfaction*. And now here I was, watching helplessly as a ginger floozy with small patches of eczema on her elbows admired my toaster. This had all gone horribly, horribly wrong.

After a long and involved discussion about the best place to position a microwave in a crowded kitchen, Matty clapped his hands together like a pleased quiz host and asked if I'd like to join them in the bedroom.

'Oh, that's okay,' I said. 'I've probably got some vacuuming to do anyway. You two go right ahead.'

He insisted, politely. I could see his eyes daring me into the experience.

'You wanted this,' they seemed to say. 'I've set it up. Now stop being such a pussy and let's just get into the bedroom and get it over with.'

Inevitably I allowed myself to be led back into the bedroom and our generous soul of a callgirl led us through the motions of an unbearably awkward and somewhat sweetly naff threeway, which was interrupted only a couple of times by the sounds of a very unhappy and confused dog howling the blues in the laundry. I'll refrain from discussing the act itself in too much detail as while I have many life ambitions, becoming the next Nikki Gemmell is not one of them, though I will mention that if you're looking for the perfect Valentine's Day gift nothing says 'I want to get close to you' quite like no-name-brand lubricant and a dental dam.

'DO YIS MIND IF I USE YER BATHROOM?'

Possibly not quite on par with the soothing sound of listening to one's parents pootling about in the kitchen drying the dinner dishes, it is nonetheless strangely comforting lying in bed hearing a prostitute use your shower. There may even be a moment of fretting that you haven't left a clean towel out, before you remember that the guest in question touches genitals for a living and may not mind sharing your Expo 88 bathroom set for a few festive minutes.

Matty and I lay in my bed regarding each other in vaguely stunned silence.

Where were we supposed to go from here? What increasingly sick, depraved scenarios would we find ourselves in as we tried to top this particular arrangement? Would we push each other further into the depths of experimental hell and end up hanging naked from door handles like Michael Hutchence? Is that how these kinds of things worked? Would I turn up on the front page of *New Weekly*—'Relatively obscure ABC scriptwriter in transgender amputee octopule daisy chain shock'?

Eventually the shower stopped and, employing an alarmingly twee technique that I would repeat in many a twisted, drawn-out relationship argument over future years, I decided that my best course of action at this juncture was to pretend to be asleep, thus avoiding any further awkwardness or possible exchange of phone numbers and promises to meet up for Hanukkah or however these sorts of barter arrangements worked. I may have even faked a delicate little snore. Matty duly followed suit. This scenario worked wonders on melting the heart of our new friend, who stood fondly at the bed's end watching us for a smidgen longer than was entirely comfortable—like a kindly grandmother musing privately to herself about how fast they grow up these days before heading out to her recliner and knitting a glove. She even became so caught up in the emotion of the moment she leaned over and whispered to us.

'*Youse two are going to sleep like angels*,' she said in hushed, sweet tones. Presumably it was all she could do to restrain herself from giving us a kiss on our cheeky little foreheads and reading us a chapter from *James and the Giant Peach*. When we'd heard her let herself out and clip-clop down to her minder's car two hundred and fifty dollars richer, we opened our eyes and looked at each other.

We should have left it at that. We should have chalked it up to experience and moved on with our lives leaving only a few minor emotional scars and a vaguely bawdy story to shriek over in moments of obscene intoxication. I don't know if *less* sex with prostitutes would have saved our already careening-out-of-control relationship, but in the end amid the chaos of perceived slights, furious arguments over money, and screaming, alcohol-fuelled street battles I doubt the two other encounters helped much. Matty and I were on a path to annihilation.

The second—months and months after our debut tryst with Mrs Ling; it took us both a while to wash the abject awkwardness from our scarred retinas and talk ourselves back into the game—was during an utterly obscene blowout weekend in Melbourne's Grand Hyatt where we indulged in the sort of idiotic orgiastic display that even Shane MacGowan would baulk at for being 'slightly over the top'. We draped ourselves all over the room with that mixed sense of daring and ownership that comes with paying ludicrous amounts of money for a hotel stay, ate club sandwiches in bed, spilt red wine on the complimentary robes and made a nuisance of ourselves with the overnight duty manager. We also—and Dear Starving Children of Africa I apologise profusely in advance for this piece of information—paid a thousand dollars for a hooker to visit our room. Perhaps it was the recklessness of being away from home that led me to believe that this would be a good idea. There was no dog to worry about, there were no gym clothes, no library books. Just a gaping suitcase trailing stay-up fishnet stockings and a torn Wheels & Dollbaby dress that made me look like an oversexed Christmas cracker. To be honest I think the only reason I was talked around—again, this man was persuasive to say the least—was an intense curiosity over what a thousand-dollar hooker might look like. Would she be seven hundred and fifty dollars more attractive than our ginger pal? Would we be paying top dollar for political debate and knock-knock jokes? Would fireworks fizz forth from her vagina on point of climax? A thousand dollars was a *lot* of money.

'Let's just stop talking about it and *book it*,' cried Matty, displaying what would eventually become an all-too-familiar enthusiasm for spending somebody else's money. And I, beholden to his spiky allure, had no choice but to comply.

The poor girl. She was lovely. She looked like Dawn from *The Office* and at the hotel-room door she regarded our two drunk, sweaty, over-eager faces with the sort of mild contempt usually seen on an *X Factor* judge directly following an off-key rendition of Lady Gaga's 'Paparazzi'.

'Hiiiiiiii,' she breathed with forced enthusiasm.

'Do come in. Can I get you a drink? Gin and tonic?' Matty was a genial host when he chose to be. He was like the Noël Coward of the prostitute set.

'I'm right, thanks.'

'Might get one myself, then.'

He veered off drunkenly to the minibar. Dawn and I regarded each other with shy, comradely smiles. I suddenly could see where this was heading. We were going to be like best girlfriends, spending the night swapping stories and giggling and occasionally pausing to lightly hit each other over the head with soft pillows. Only instead of tagging her in Facebook photos I would pay her a grand to have sex with my boyfriend while I sat on a chair drinking glasses of champagne. What could be more bonding?

• • •

The final encounter—and I say that with no small sense of weariness, as even writing about it makes me feel tired and slightly nauseous—was a year later, after an eight-hour drinking session (there's a pattern here, yes) at the Retreat Hotel in Brunswick, during which time Matty and I had wondered aloud what it might be like to have a threeway with a male friend. The obligatory 'Which of my mates would you want to fuck?'/'No, which of your mates would you be *okay* with me fucking?' conversation followed, along with a long list of people we could ask who wouldn't laugh us out of town. We then undulated back to his bungalow and tittered to ourselves for a long and involved while before he lunged for the Yellow Pages and called for a male escort.

'Matty, you *mustn't*,' I murmured in the unprotesting voice of someone quite prepared to see how this next faintly ridiculous turn of events would unfold.

Male prostitutes—the final frontier.

And the one we eventually got was on his 'L' plates.

'I'm a bit nervous,' he confessed as he arrived at the bungalow, all sweaty palms and apologetic smiles. Which is exactly what you want in a male whore, isn't it? A bashful type, eyes downward, looking for all the world like he'd spend the rest of the evening politely losing games of backgammon and making fruit whips with Matty's housemates in the communal kitchen. Lord knows where these people get their licences. Is there a TAFE course?

Our guest perched uncomfortably in the doorway. I sensed his trepidation and flew into mother-hen mode.

'Would you like a cup of tea?' I proffered brightly, while Matty shot me a what-the-fuck-do-you-think-you're-doing look. How could I help it? The poor, slightly built manchild appeared to have wandered off the set of *Oliver!* and into his worst nightmare.

Nonetheless, we persevered. We were practically professional perverts by this stage. At any rate, we were clearly at least two times more experienced than our perspiring, terrified escort. It was all I could do not to take him by the hand and murmur, 'There there, dear heart. We'll look after you.' It was like having sex with Bambi.

I was bold after my two previous encounters, imperfect though they had been. I took charge of the situation and pointed out who should go where and at what exact moment. I may have even haggled. I'm not proud of it.

Our new friend—bless his face, he should have been nominated for a bravery award—duly mucked in ('all hands on deck now, there's a good lad') and things seemed to be progressing nicely until at one point I looked up and Matty wasn't there. He had just . . . disappeared. Further investigation found him brooding outside the doorway of the bungalow, smoking cigarettes and scowling. He couldn't handle it, he said, seeing me with another guy. It was all fine *in theory*. But there we were, right in front of him, in his bed, on his sheets. It was enough to make a man fair lose his erection, which is precisely what had happened. And now he was furious with himself. No, wait, he was furious with me. Or our hapless visitor, who was by this stage standing naked and awkward in the corner of the room desperately wishing he was at home with mum and dad watching *Hey Hey It's Saturday*.

'I could . . . go,' he offered helpfully, and Matty, awash with feeling, stirred up and sickened and upset in a way he'd never imagined, dismissed him with a curt nod. I don't remember our escort getting dressed. To this day there must be some random neighbour in Brunswick who in 2004 bore witness to a shrieking naked twenty-something running from a house and into the night.

I felt ridiculous. Vulnerable. I lashed out.

'I thought you *wanted* to try it.'

'I did!'

'So what happened?'

Matty, who had seen it all. Matty, who had lived a life of girls and drugs and fist fights. Matty, who talked up the beautiful knife edge of our existence but was suddenly wishing the whole damned thing had never happened and we could go back to being a normal couple who did things like going to the laundromat or eating toasted pides at Ray on a Sunday morning with the papers spread-eagled out in front of us.

He was nearly in tears.

'It was too . . . *real*.'

We stayed together for a while after that but to be honest the whole notion of dangerous experimentation was growing increasingly hollow. I still loved that terrible glint in Matty's eye when everything was about to get wild, when the ground would disappear beneath us and we'd wake up two days later in his dark and sticky bedroom above the Chinese restaurant on Sydney Road, crying and apologising and swearing to each other we'd never let it get so fucked up again. And then we did, of course, we let the cycle continue, because we were both damaged little flowers who seemed to bring out the worst in each other. We never mentioned what had happened in the bungalow or joked about paying for whores again, and eventually I called time on the relationship. Or he did. The details are hazy. There were some snotty, undignified tears on the carpet of my Northcote home and somebody slammed a door and that was it.

He ended up with someone even crazier than me and I briefly fell for a dreamboat with a mohawk who embodied calm and sunshine, and after some months of snarling and spitting at each other from a safe distance Matty and I decided it was best to drift apart and cease contact altogether. Occasionally I would look at his blog and read between the lines of all the long, poetic posts he published late at night. ('We ate croissants and cheese, and drank red wine though it was barely 11 am. We felt very French. We were sophisticated. I told her we were two halves of a broken star.') I wrote a story for *The Age* about our painful time at a music festival and he bombarded me with angry texts for an entire afternoon before calling a truce.

'I guess you have the right,' he conceded eventually, 'to tell our story how you want.'

There's only so many times you can break your own heart with the helpless, fumbling, all-consuming humanness of sexuality before you realise that there's something profoundly odd about the entire race itself. We seek out these pleasures of the flesh in such a sweet, confused, hypothetical fashion. I had wanted to live in the moment, and yet plunged into some sort of depraved and slightly comedic fantasy world instead. I was over it. And aside from that, more than three visits with prostitutes probably qualifies you as a bona fide pervert and while I may be many things I'm pretty certain I'm not one. I just have a curiosity about human beings, my world, and musical theatre as a genre, and I'm fully determined the latter won't be getting me into any further trouble.

From: Marieke Hardy
Subject: Travels
Date: 9 November 2010 11:23:45 AM
To: ****@gmail.com

Hi Matty
Long time no anything. I see from your blog that you're overseas and playing music – I hope it's proving a fulfilling and creative experience.

This may seem a bit of a left-of-field email but I'll just plunge on regardless. I don't even know if this is still your address, so forgive me if I'm shouting into the ether.

I am writing a book at the moment, of autobiographical short stories. Given the fairly heady years we spent together, you will likely appear in a couple. I understand the Meredith story I wrote for The Age was fairly confronting for you, so I wanted to not only give you a heads-up well in advance, but also to give you the chance to respond to the pieces. I'm happy to print those responses and any exchanges we may have regarding potentially diverse rememberings of shared encounters. This may sit oddly with you, but I'm hoping that as a writer you appreciate the process. I know that we see the past through different eyes, but believe we both have a right to tell it in our own way.

Please don't fear that the pieces will be some sort of character assassination, either – for some reason I always end up as the worst behaved person in my stories.

Safe travels
Marieke

From: ****@gmail.com
Subject: Re: Re: Travels
Date: 9 November 2010 2:15:59 PM
To: Marieke Hardy

No problemo, ma'am. If I have a chance to respond, that'd be ace biscuits.

It's nice to hear from you, lovely. Let me know what you need and when.

Travelling and playing music is so beautiful I can't give it justice. I've discovered a society of gypsies, and I finally feel at home.

Portland, OR, is like a larger Daylesford. You'd seriously love it.

Okeypoke. Just stay in touch and let me know. I understand a lot more now. Last year's piece came at a particularly bad time for me. Now, like you, I am not afraid.

Hope you're all good, missb.

Oh, and I'm still a rude punner, so . . . Heady Years. hehe.

Okbye

x

From: Marieke Hardy
Subject: Re: Travels
Date: 15 November 2010 3:41:18 PM
To: ****@gmail.com

Okay then, deep breaths . . .

I have no idea what you're going to make of this. I hope you find the funny bits funny, at the very least. As faintly absurd as this time was in our lives, there is something nice about looking back on it so fondly.

As previously stated, very open to your thoughts.

Enjoy your gypsy roamings.

m.

From: ****@gmail.com
Subject: Re: Travels
Date: 15 November 2010 6:37:16 PM
To: Marieke Hardy

Hey ma'am,

I'm sitting in a kitchen in Seattle. It's real strange here. Coldhearted. People don't talk to each other. I try and grin cheekily on the street, but I never know if I'm going to get stabbed or bought a coffee. Anyway. It’s a funny place to read about all this.

I wasn’t sure what you were going to write about. And, I guess, this may be the one time I see what our relationship meant to you. So, in a way, in a long, distant, way – as you might write – it saddens me. I was never a fist-fightin’, whore-fuckin’ troublemaker. I was in love at the time. I fed off and fed the energy that came out of the girl I fell madly, head over heels in love with. The girl that I naively thought felt the same. But that’s okay. Please don’t think this paragraph is written with anything other than a wistful sigh. There is no pain, anger or hurt. Just my truth.

I liked your piece. Factually, ah, bendy, but I liked it. And I see through your eyes in it. That’s what I meant about the love thing. I never saw myself as trouble. I saw myself as devoted, and willing to try, though drink and hurt I did along the way. It’s all good now. I wish I was more writey tonight, but I’m so head spun by being on a tour when I don’t even really play music . . .

I'm so Bukowski every time you write of me. I'm going to take that as a compliment. And, I don't think anyone can read between the lines o' my blog. Ask Dave the Scot. I just may not be the person you remember. Or the person you think I am. That's a real shame to me. That you don't know me at all.

Anyways, thanks for asking and sharing. I have no problem whatsoever with this trip you're on. Do as you do. Write as you write. My only criticism, as a writer, would be, if you're going to share – then don't hold back. Because, it seems you want to share Marieke the caricature, when the soul of the Marieke that I knew, in dark, hard times, well, she was a real person. And a lovely one at that.

Much love, missb. Hope you find what it is you're looking for.
Matty x

The write stuff

In March 2010 my friend Michaela and I started a monthly literary salon called Women of Letters. It would be, we claimed grandly, 'an homage to the lost art of letter-writing' (we knew it was correct to use the form 'an' before a word starting with a silent 'h' even though doing so in public usually resulted in being left alone at the bar) and bring together five women from various fields who would each pen and read aloud a letter about a topic of our choosing. During a twenty-minute interval, we would encourage our audience to write letters of their own to whomsoever they chose. We would scatter the venue with aerogrammes, postcards, pens, paper and envelopes. We would have a big wooden postbox. And we would provide real, honest-to-god stamps, so that attendees could actually post their letters and someone, somewhere would one day in the near future receive them in the mail.

Michaela and I debated a great deal over how the letter-writing part of the afternoon would work.

'People get embarrassed about audience participation,' I pointed out. 'They'll think we're stupid.'

We workshopped ways to get the crowd excited about the idea of not talking to their friends for twenty minutes and writing a cheery little note about where they were and what they'd been up to instead. It would be a hard sell. People liked to chat at intervals. They liked to lean back in their chair and exhale languidly and pick apart everything that had occurred in the first half of the show. They certainly wouldn't want to sit still and write letters.

'We need to try it regardless,' replied my bespectacled conspirator, 'and just see what happens.'

Against all odds it worked, and we have been dumb-lucky enough to spend our hobby time putting on regular events up and down the east coast of the country. These days the interval is almost my favourite part of the day, as our five readers file from the stage to the soundtrack of '60s pop records and I look out over the room and see three hundred or so heads bent over, focused on scribbling missives to faraway friends. More often than not I go home at day's end slightly drunk and clumsily upend the wooden postbox over my living room floor, spilling out all the words and secrets and enclosed notes in a dizzy jumble. I look at them for a long time and think about who might be receiving them and how they may shape a stranger's morning in some significant fashion. On Mondays I post them, stuffing everything into the big red postbox on Sydney Road in happy fistfuls.

That we have somehow created a position for ourselves

as conduit, a bridge between a shy audience member and their mother, or ex-lover, or erstwhile primary school teacher ('Dear Mrs Abercrombie, I hope you don't mind but I found your postal address on my iPhone . . .') is a wonderful feeling. It's doubtful we'll be receiving knighthoods from Australia Post but it's difficult not to feel as though you're part of something very special when you consider that at least one hundred people who may not have otherwise received a personal letter in their letterbox will now be doing so just because Michaela and I needed a public place to get drunk on a Sunday afternoon.

Perhaps it's because I was conceived back in the day when my father's only job was being a mascot for Australia Post airmail, but I love getting letters. Doesn't everybody? Saying you like receiving personal letters in the post is like stating that you rather enjoy breathing, or having ears on either side of your head: it's taken as a given, and not to be used as a quirky character trait to lure in members of the opposite sex on dating sites. Even seeing the spidery, in-my-day-we-sent-letters-via-donkey-and-wolfpack handwriting of an elderly relative can send a cheap frisson when indulging in a dressing-gowned visit to the front gate.

Because they do, letters, don't they? They exist in a tangible, rich way that their cheap, instant-gratification-grasping distant cousin emails can only dream of. There are too many vague, unfulfilled promises in emails, too much that passes us by in a manic rush of deleting and copying and pasting and BCC-ing. A letter is a long and leisurely afternoon lying naked on a picnic rug eating a Flake.

I once held a passionate discourse with a feline-eyed slice of wonderful via email. Outside of a brief and not unexciting handholding session in a country carpark, that was about as far as our romance progressed. Everything else was charted in breathless late-night paragraphs, pressing 'send' and then waiting agonising hours for a response. I didn't have a mobile phone back then so we didn't text. He was in a relationship so I wasn't able to write postcards. Had I not printed out our correspondence in a tearful burst of sentimentality it all would have disappeared in the great hard-drive crash of 2004 and I would only have ever recalled his prose in vague fragments. And what a pity it would have been, to lose that sense of urgent subtext and collection of our beautiful, shared, misspent memory.

Letters make you wait. Letters make you patient. You can hold a letter in your hand, kiss it, inhale the tobacco aroma of its author. You can keep it in a shoebox. You can cry over it and smear the text with your salty emoting.

In the late 1990s, I went on what could only be called a letter-writing binge. I wrote to everybody. I wrote to Joan Kirner and Jeff Kennett and John Cain. I wrote a love letter to the now sadly deceased ABC journalist Paul Lyneham (who penned a handwritten response which included the rather bemused: 'most viewers only write to complain so supportive comments like yours are highly valued'). I wrote to Bill Bryson and David Sedaris and Michael J Fox. I wrote hate mail to Aden Ridgeway and those three other Australian Democrat jerkoffs when they banded together and bloodlessly shunted the bright, brilliant Senator Natasha Stott Despoja. Some of the people I wrote to responded. Some didn't. A small handful very likely called the authorities who to this day I expect still have me on file.

I printed and kept these letters in a plastic ringbinder where they sat for over ten years. When during an idle moment Michaela asked me to think about topics for future Women of Letters events I remembered this folder and dug it out. I had a sense that back then I'd been a passionate, engaged, optimistic correspondent—a young freedom fighter, ready to bring forth change on a worldwide level. What I didn't understand was that I'd been a super pest, bordering on mildly autistic, with the frightening self-confidence of a heavily medicated Charlie Sheen. ('I am on a drug, it's called Charlie Sheen. It's not available because if you try it once you will die, your face will melt off and your children will weep over your exploded body.')

15.7.1998

Dear Sir or Madam,
I am writing with regards to a recent White Wings commercial involving two little girls sitting on a bench at school comparing play lunches.

The original commercial involved one rather limp blonde child singing the praises of her saccharine mother's view towards cake products ('My mother says this . . . my mother thinks that . . .' etc), while our feisty heroine in pigtails rolls her eyes

> *before delivering the knock-out punchline . . . 'So does mine—but she's got a life.' . . .*

Yes, this is really what it looks like at first glance: a letter to White Wings about one of their television advertisements. If you presumed these sorts of letters were written by tremblingly furious pensioners who only paused their lengthy diatribes to spoon a modest amount of cat food into their spit-flecked mouth, think again.

> *. . . This was such a great commercial, filled with sassiness and attitude. Yet the company recently seems to have chickened out, cutting the final line, leaving the two little saps agreeing smilingly as they tuck into their White Wings cakes . . .*

Cue incandescent rage.

> *. . . Why have you done this? You have taken all the life out of your advertisement with one cut. Whoever the big cheese with cold feet is, they should have their head examined . . .*

Use of the phrases 'big cheese' and 'cold feet' in such close succession would indicate this letter was clearly written with toothpick in mouth whilst waiting for Big Moe and the boys to do a little bada bing with some violin cases or whatever it was gangsters from 1950s cinema got up to in their spare time when they weren't slapping their ladyfriends meatily on the backside. If the Pettingill family is ever looking for a new matriarch they need search no further.

I mean, really.
Disappointedly,
Marieke Hardy

'I mean, really.' I was twenty-two years old in 1998 and already sounding like the sort of stitched-up biddy who distrusts the coloureds 'because they hum to themselves while they sew'. Nothing like rounding off the argument with a motherly tut to really make a large corporation sit up and take notice.

Interestingly enough, far from writing me off as a complete nutjob who pays a worrying amount of attention to the intricacies of their television commercials, some poor soul at Uncle Tobys sat down and patiently dictated a response.

Dear Ms Hardy,
Thank you for contacting us in regard to one of our products . . .

Now I'm no Nancy Drew, but I strongly suspect that the consumer relations department may have been phoning this one in. 'One of our products'?? IT WAS THE WHITE WINGS CAKE COMMERCIAL AND YOU AND I BOTH KNOW IT UNCLE TOBY IF INDEED YOU ARE MY REAL UNCLE.

> . . . Uncle Tobys is a company that takes pride in the quality of our products and services and appreciate the time you have taken to contact us . . .

. . . 'particularly since the rest of your busy day must be filled with pressing appointments for biting the heads off pigeons at Flinders Street Station and standing outside the window of random restaurants drooling onto the glass and shrieking MISTER DONUT ATE MY SOUL at startled diners.'

> . . . and the interest you have taken in our company's products.
>
> It is only feedback from consumers that enables us to measure the ongoing and long-term quality of our products.
>
> Please accept our complimentary parcel of products for your enjoyment. We trust that you will continue to be a valued White Wings customer.
>
> Yours sincerely,
> Incomprehensible scribble
> CONSUMER RELATIONS DEPARTMENT

And there it was, delivered by a likely wary courier ('don't make eye contact, and don't let her touch your skin'): a cardboard box full of Uncle Tobys quality foodstuffs. Cynics among you may think that my sole reason for writing these deranged missives was to score free comestibles. It's untrue. I swear it. Symptom of a strange and lonely headspace it may be, but letter-writing of that type is often driven by a burning passion to right a perceived wrong. Seeing that White Wings advertisement had stirred something significant and furious in me, the perception of an error that I felt needed to be immediately redressed. I didn't want free muesli bars. I wanted them to *change the commercial back to the way it was when I liked it.*

> *20.9.1998*
>
> *Sax International*
> *5/278 Ferntree Gully Road*
> *Notting Hill 3149*
>
> *To Whom It May Concern,*
> *This is just a short note to congratulate you on an excellent product. I came across your stay-on colourstick quite by accident . . . my local chemist didn't stock Revlon, which I have used for some time . . .*

Bam! Take that, Sax International! I haven't always been your bitch! That's right, I sleep around! Heed my feelings!

> *. . . and was told to give Sax a try. Since then, I have worn your lipstick out about three times . . .*

Three, no less. Obviously I felt I needed that extra outing to truly ensure the odds-on experiment had proven successful.

> *. . . and each time have found it to be absolutely wonderful. For someone like me whose beauty routines are strictly low-maintenance . . .*

What led me to briefly and mysteriously channel the spirit of Ita Buttrose with that particular sentence remains unknown. I have never uttered aloud the words 'someone like me whose beauty routines are strictly low-maintenance' in my life. It's as though I have just arrived in a foreign country and, unable to speak the language, parked myself in front of a television screening nothing but commercials for the Ponds Institute on high rotation. Which suggests I would later weave the terms 'nine out of ten trial participants agree' and 'clinical tests prove' effortlessly throughout the letter.

> *. . . it is a pleasure to find a lipstick I can just put on and forget about . . . least to mention, not having to 'top up' after eating meals . . .*

Good to add the verb 'eating' in there lest the good people at the Sax factory had pondered exactly what it was I may have been doing with my meals. Staring mindlessly at them, perhaps? Cavorting naked around them in an ancient Wiccan ritual and/or smearing them upon my flushed and perspiring torso? Nobody likes 'topping up' (inverted commas model's own) after that sort of activity.

. . . The second time I wore colourstick, I ate oysters for dinner (how terribly decadent this all sounds) . . .

Note wry self-deprecating comment upon one's lavish lifestyle lest Sax HQ presume one is unaware of how dreadfully Gatsby it all is. Oysters! For dinner! Next thing she'll be telling us she's mainlining gin and trading eloquent barbs with Alexander Woollcott at the Algonquin.

. . . and was amazed to find that after the meal my lipstick looked absolutely untouched.

I am certainly not someone who writes letters like this often . . .

Liar.

. . . in fact, I hardly ever wear makeup at all, so I'm quite unqualified to comment on professional textures and standards . . .

This is one of the most intensely obnoxious sentences I have ever written in my life. And I once wrote a feature film called *Digital Duck* about a duck who could surf the internet.

. . . However I thought it was worth writing to let you know that you have found a very satisfied customer who will be purchasing more of your products in future.
Cheers,
Marieke Josephine Hardy

I'm sure Sax appreciated the classy additional touch of my middle name in the sign-off. 'We're dealing with a real lady here!' they must have whistled to themselves in awe. 'No wonder she has no time to "top up" after her bacchanalian feasts!'

The Sax piece was an interesting letter to find as it proved that I wasn't simply a burning ball of indignation, firing off angry missives to whomsoever captured my disapproving eye. No, I was also a generous soul, spreading corporate love and goodwill to those deserving. This character trait continued years later when I personally crafted a card—there was glue stick and glitter involved—for the nice company (Uncle Tobys again—there's a fair chance they had a photocopied picture of me up in reception with the words 'UNDER ANY CIRCUMSTANCES' written somewhere on it by this stage) who distributed my favourite breakfast cereal, Oats Temptations. 'It's so exciting to put a hand into the box and retrieve the flavour that will shape my morning!!' I wrote enthusiastically and dementedly in bright green texta.

30.9.1998

Dear Ms Hardy
RE: STAY-ON COLOURSTICK
Thank you so much for your letter received last week regarding our SAX Stay-On Colourstick. It is great to hear you love the product.

It is very satisfying for Sax International to receive positive letters from the public. For your efforts in writing to us, please find enclosed with our compliments an 'Earthy Me' Colourstick and an 'Earthy Nude' Stay-On Lipliner.

We are confident you will enjoy wearing them.

Kind regards,
A Arvan
Sales and Marketing Coordinator

The process of sifting through the ringbinder of my old correspondence was both horrifying and curious. Who was this person, compelled to engage in lengthy postal debate with faceless strangers about lipsticks and advertising campaigns? What drove her beyond the step of complaining loudly at dinner tables to actually sitting down and crafting meaningless long-winded written diatribes?

September 15th, 1999

Dear Mariek [*sic*]
Thank you for contacting Ocean Spray.

As indicated in our phone conversation, please find enclosed the information you requested. We hope you will find it helpful. We appreciate your interest and will continue to work to bring you the finest products available.

Sincerely,
Mary
Consumer Representative

Mortifyingly, this letter reveals that I had taken my love of food and drink a step further and actually called the Ocean Spray offices to have a chat with them about one of their products, presumably their range of delicious cranberry juices. Given my state of mind in 1999—I was by that stage living alone in the country and had seen a demon standing next to my bed—it was likely done at three in the morning on the consumer hotline and lasted for about seven hours, with brief intervals for bouts of noisy sobbing. I don't doubt Mary still wakes up in the middle of the night on occasion drenched in sweat and screaming my name.

Finding the Ocean Spray reply in my letters folder was the equivalent of waking up after a night on Stilnox to find two entire roast chicken carcasses and a dead hooker on the floor of the bedroom. It was an indication that I took my interest in products and marketing that tiny step too far.

Politicians were a focal point of my deranged pen too. Ex-governor-general Bill Hayden clearly felt the full force of my wrath when he seized the occasion of a defamation case involving author Bob Ellis and ludicrous political duo Tony Abbott and Peter Costello to make some fairly salacious comments regarding former prime minister Paul Keating's private life:

26.10.1998

Mr. Hayden,
Are you quite mad??? . . .

A fair enquiry to be certain, guaranteed to capture the attention of even the most uncurious reader. 'Am I mad? Well, this seems like a correspondent ready to engage in a robust intellectual dialogue with neither preconceived notions nor judgement. Please, do go on!'

> *. . . Your recent behaviour re: the Bob Ellis libel case sadly leaves me certain that time has left you a very bitter man when it comes to the Keating era . . .*

Hardy Psychology 101. Please note that even Bill Hayden's Wikipedia page clearly states, 'He had a particular animosity towards Paul Keating.' Why I was congratulating myself on pointing out a fact that had been freely available to the greater public for over fifteen years is anybody's guess. I'm looking forward very much to finding the letter I wrote to the people of Berlin excitedly informing them that they are now free to roam about their city unimpeded by large concrete barriers.

> *. . . In future, please confine your revolting childishness to the privacy of your home, and stick your archaic policies with it.*
>
> *People like you, sir, make me ashamed to support the ALP . . .*

So ashamed, in fact, that I will sign the letter by using a pseudonym.

Stacie Mistysyn (Ms)

Those with a particular love of late-1980s pop culture might note that Stacie Mistysyn is the name of the actress who played attractively passionate student Caitlin Ryan in children's series *Degrassi Junior High*. Whether or not she'd approve of some rabid idiot from Melbourne sending letters to political figures under her name is yet to be ascertained. My guess is she'd probably despise Bill Hayden and congratulate me on my forthright approach.

Interestingly, Bill Hayden responded to my letter, bringing to mind the mathematical puzzle 'if one person with too much time on their hands meets another person with too much time on their hands, how many snippy, self-serving letters will they write before one of them suffers an aneurysm?' He responded by photocopying a whole lot of articles with titles like BILL HAYDEN'S 'DEVASTATING' TRIAL BY MEDIA, LABOR MAKES HAYDEN PAY FOR 'DEFECTING' and WHY HAYDEN'S CRITICS GOT IT WRONG and then put them in an envelope along with a little note that simply read 'With Compliments: The Hon. Bill Hayden, AC' which is a fairly decent and admirable sort of 'go fuck yourself', really.

The ringbinder of shame proved I made beginner's mistakes, of course. When boorish shock jock Stan Zemanek was still alive and hosting daytime talk show *Beauty and the Beast* I—like a fool, like a fool—bought into his red-faced baiting of the pious left:

2.2.1999

Dear Sir or Madam,
I am writing with regards to a channel ten program aired at one thirty pm on Tuesday, the second of February . . .

To be precise. Jesus christ. Nobody should be that pedantic about dates and times outside of Emmett 'Doc' Brown and/or the entire Mayan population.

. . . titled Beauty and the Beast. *It involves a male host (Stan Zemanek) and a panel of female celebrities solving viewer dilemmas and commenting upon general media . . .*

Oh, *that Beauty and the Beast* from one thirty pm, Tuesday February 2nd. Way to clear it up, Cleary McClearenstein.

. . . I have been watching for fifteen minutes now and am absolutely appalled. No more than five minutes into the program the host had not only called the women 'pooches', but had also told a panelist she could never be mistaken for a boy 'with those tits'. He then began lewdly referring to a necklace she was wearing as 'balls around her neck', and addressed each panelist as 'darling', pin-pointing Julia Morris as a 'lesbian' because she had a short haircut . . .

Let's leave aside for a moment the fact that at the time of writing I was hosting a radio program on community radio station Triple R called *Best of the Brat*, which involved a segment named 'Celebrity Rooter'. During this particular segment musicians would play their top five songs to fuck to, whilst talking lewdly and openly about intercourse. Yet I obviously had—and still have—my limits, at least when it came to daytime television and other such moral bastions. We all do, which is why sordid little cockstains like Alan Jones are allowed to pass judgement on the behaviour of young women in burqas whilst simultaneously being arrested for acts of indecency in public toilet blocks. No glass house left unshattered.

Whether I simply held no faith that a letter from a twenty-three-year-old screenwriter would carry much weight with the bigwigs (or 'big cheeses', for the White Wings employees among you), the following paragraph proves that I was only moments away from being escorted off to the Zelda Fitzgerald Center for Slightly Hysterical Ladies.

> *. . . I am complaining about this program not only as a woman . . .*

Vagina? Present!

> *. . . but as a mother. I have a sick eight-year-old daughter at home with me today, and felt that at the very least I could sit her in front of some harmless daytime television . . .*

That's right, in order to rouse what I felt were the just and proper responses from the Channel Ten authorities I invoked a fictional child. Please note that this is the exact sort of behaviour that makes the baby Jesus cry.

> *. . . Harmless indeed! If I had any idea of the revolting innuendo and sexist banter that was to be aired, I would have rented a video. As it was, I just turned the television off. And it will stay off until you consider running some sensible daytime television, as opposed to this disgusting rubbish.*
> *Yours furiously,*
> *Stacie Mistysyn (Mrs)*

So my whole non-existent family was being punished for the sins of Stan Zemanek. No television until the entire network sits up and takes notice, invisible children!

Not long after that Stan got a brain tumour (presumably unrelated to one particular letter from an angry fake housewife) and appeared in lots of women's magazines looking sad and bald with his teary wife and headlines like NOBODY KNOWS MY STAN LIKE I DO and I felt briefly sorry for him. Which quickly passed—he was a bad egg and besides which he never replied to my heartfelt outpourings. Won't someone think of the (fictional) children?

That *Beauty and the Beast* letter began a whole cunning series written with the intention of 'hoodwinking the respondent'. Obviously in my feverish state I was obsessed with the idea of fooling whomever may be unlucky enough to receive my latest missive and fashioned my pieces accordingly. I created dead husbands and injured pets and traumatised children. I pretended to live in bush huts and government housing and Toorak mansions. And occasionally I attempted to make a political organisation sit up and take notice by coming across like an enthused fan suffering a sustained brain injury.

21.01.1999

Dear Young Liberals,
I have just heard about youre new ideas for the Young Liberals and I am thinking about joining. I heard it on channel nine news a week or so ago but it took me until today to write to you. That is not to say that I have not been thinking about it because I have been thinking about it very much. My local Pastor says I could be an excelent person in politics as I have very strong opinons on a number of topics.

First though I have a queston for you:

1: Is there an age requirement for people who want to join the Young Liberals? (dont worry I am sixteen and not to young)

b: Do I have to live in Queensland to join the Queensland Young Liberals? I am asking this because while I live in Victoria from what I here the Queensland Young Liberals seem to get a lot more done than the Victorian Young Liberals who I have not read to much about.

c: If I join the Young Liberals can I have a say in what we talk about and so on because of the topcs raised on the news I have some opinions about.

I have been thinking about a few of the ideas. One is the 'G' plate for older drivers which I think is a very very good idea. My grandma is 73 and when she was driving I found it quite embarrsing. I would lie down in the back seat so that no0one I would know would see my driving with her as her driving was very bad and I didnt want people to think that maybe one day I would drive like that to. As she is now in a nursing home this is no longer a very big problem however I am sure other people would like for some law like this to be past to save them the same embarrassment from their friends when they are forced to drive with old people who everyone knows cant drive.

Also signs that should be in english would be good to. If people are going to come to austraila they need to learn the language as well as speak it properly. If they just come here and we let them put up signs in there own language they will never learn how to join in our societry.

Also I dont think that having the politicians in Star Trek uniforms is a very good idea to. I dont know if this was a joke idea but it is not good to put it with youre other ideas because people will think that the other ideas are jokes when really they are good ideas which should be listened to and not for people to think they are jokes. So maybe it would be good to write to the papers and tell them that the Star Trek idea was a joke so they can print it so people will know to.

Anyway I think John Howard is a very good prime minster and I am glad he won the election even if it wasn't by very much. He has some good ideas to and I will write more about that after I join.

Anyway you guys are cool! Please write back soon!!!!
Sincerely from
Stacie Mistysyn.

Poor Stacie Mistysyn, moniker used in vain yet again, this time with the sole purpose of making fun of the Queensland Young Liberals. There was possibly some kind of stoner logic attached to writing a fan letter in the style of Snooki from *Jersey Shore*. No doubt I had pictured the right-wing twits at the Young Liberal headquarters gathering around to read with worried frowns, musing aloud that if this was the sort of halfwit fan they were attracting with their policies perhaps they should probably just rethink the whole thing, or even give up altogether.

The hobby (quest? compulsion?) of writing to companies soon ebbed, no doubt much to the combined relief of the managing directors at Uncle Tobys, Sax International and Ocean Spray, and I instead wrote to new friends. I wrote to wharfies I'd met during the MUA dispute. I wrote to distant relatives, and admired artists, and people whose stories in the press had moved me. The frothing mania of changing the world, one stamp at a time, receded as I grew older, replaced simply by a need to reach out to another human being via a medium more thoughtful, more palpable, than a 3 am text message or dashed-off gmail. There was love in a letter. There was a heart. At Women of Letters shows I too now bent over an aerogramme, glass of wine abandoned as I scrawled across the page. I wanted to belong.

After a relationship broke down I gently attempted to mend bridges and build a gentler future by writing one long, self-reflective, blameless letter per week. It was my wish that when my ex-partner held my words in his hands he would forgive my many mistakes, and sense the impassioned hope between every line of my poor penmanship. That he would appreciate that I'd taken the time to sit down and write him a letter, because no electronic missive could convey the sentiment of our years together, nor possibly help us find common ground. And I didn't use a pseudonym, and I didn't create fictional children or complain about a broken or tasteless product.

I just told him I loved him and put it in the post; he could read it as often or as little as he liked.

Forevz

This is a cancer story that has some jokes in it, so if you think perhaps that's in poor taste it's probably best that you put this book down and spend a long and absorbing hour listening to Don McLean's song 'Driedel' and talking to your friends about how deeply meaningful it is instead of reading further. This is a cancer story that has some jokes in it mostly because the main person in the story who has cancer is the funniest person I know. I never intended to write a funny cancer story because cancer is, by nature, inherently unamusing. Michael Cera is yet to star in a feelgood buddy cancer comedy featuring dick jokes and pop culture references ('Hey Chemo-Sabe, if I radiotherapy my balls will I become like a porno Peter Parker and shoot spiderwebs instead of semen?'). Comedian Bill Hicks had some fairly poignant stand-up shows after being diagnosed with terminal pancreatic cancer but even then he didn't necessarily make jokes about his condition, nor were many people in his audience even aware that he was dying. If you Google the words 'cancer jokes'—look, we all have our dark evenings at home alone trying to find distractions from the recesses of our respective souls and I'll thank you not to judge—one of the first websites that appears is the rather timidly titled 'Are You Ready For Cancer Jokes?' It manages one—just one—joke (the clumsily worded 'Q: What do you call a person who has a compulsion to get lymphoma over and over again? A: A lymphomaniac!' Look forward to reading this one aloud from a Christmas cracker next December) before retreating rapidly, hands raised in surrender, with five lengthy paragraphs explaining that the person who runs the website has *actually been diagnosed with prostate cancer* so drop your burning torches, cease your poisonous emails, we're all dealing with our healing process in different ways and laughter/medicine, so forth.

Gen was the first person I knew to get sick, properly sick, and it hit our group of friends like a train. We were in our early thirties, still dancing around the concept of recklessness, dawdling irresponsibly with commitment like bored, aimless teenagers. There were carbon copy nights of hard drinking where we would inevitably end up back at Blair and Angie's house in East Brunswick at three o'clock in the morning, talking too loudly and attempting to crump and knocking over furniture. It was a ten-year summer; nobody could be bothered getting pregnant and everybody kept going to gigs and sticking powders up their noses and nothing really changed. There was the lazy expectation that with any luck it would stay like this forever. We were old enough to know better. We just didn't feel like knowing better.

People our age didn't get cancer. Grownups got cancer. Friends of parents, distant aunts, paper thin grandmothers with a plethora of pre-existing ailments. Or that one sad and strange kid from primary school who kept turning up to class, month after month, with considerably less hair and a big brave scared smile, until one day they didn't turn up anymore and the principal said something adult in assembly about happier places and peace of mind that nobody really understood.

Cancer was maudlin and sentimental. Cancer was in *Beaches*. Cancer was a dull reminder that we wouldn't be spared those difficult, painful feelings of process and grief the rest of the adult world had to experience. That it had happened to Gen—a woman whose brassy, milk-curdling laugh was so robustly impossible to ignore she and I were often asked to leave restaurants so other diners could continue their meals in peace—was simply absurd. She was an independent, forthright, guitar-playing smart alec. A band she had been in years before were briefly the darlings of Triple J and teenagers had lined up around the block to see her play. On stage she was all snarl and sass and 1980s prom dresses. She was known for her quick wit and collection of sequinned windcheaters. In the days of Myspace she had competed with our friend Glenn over accumulating online friends and with concerted effort had locked in over one thousand in a week. She was brash and infuriating and somebody you always wanted to be around.

She had called me directly from the doctor's office.

'They found a lump,' she said in a flat, dull voice. 'It's big. I know it's cancer. I just *know*.'

It was three days before her thirty-sixth birthday. She had been freaking out about the milestone, gently, in that self-deprecating, self-conscious way we all had of facing birthdays in our thirties. We had been making jokes about adult nappies and jailbait boyfriends who looked at us blankly when we referenced generational things like Mudhoney and Joan Kirner. We were planning our annual liquor-sodden picnic in the park, where we would toast each other, lushly and repeatedly, and watch from half-lidded sprawlings on the grass while the children of our friends beat a piñata senseless.

Now all of a sudden the party was on hold and Gen was sitting on my couch sobbing and I was trying to half-heartedly reassure her that everybody had lumpy bosoms and it was only recently that my GP had had a prod around my décolletage and bluntly pronounced it 'one of the lumpiest damn chests I've ever encountered'.

Even talking about cancer felt hollow and Hallmark, like we were faking sincerity in some overblown daytime soap opera.

'Everything's going to be okay,' I heard myself saying to Gen in a high shrill voice. 'You're going to be okay. We'll get through this.' Given another half hour without a script I feared I would soon slip into excruciating desk calendar quotes and a montage set to the music of Joe Cocker and Jennifer Warnes's 'Up Where We Belong' involving the two of us running along a beach in slow motion.

There were tests, of course. There had to be, it was apparently the regulation thing for people with obscenely lumpy bosoms. I met with Gen and her family at the Royal Melbourne to get the results, all of us full of nervous energy and optimism. We did the crossword and made jokes about the trite photocopied posters advertising African drumming workshops for chemo patients. I imagined the oncologist laughing in our faces as he tore up the test findings, promising with chuckles how he would regale his fellow cancer specialists with the tale of this buffoon from Northcote who had wasted his entire morning falsely believing she had breast cancer.

'Wait 'til I tell the guys you thought *that* lump was *cancer*!' I pictured him saying, with matey nudges in the ribs of a giggling breast care nurse.

After an interminable wait, we were ushered into a windowless room. A clumsy young man in a too-short tie introduced himself, saying he was a student doctor and was it alright with us if he sat in on the consultation 'for learning purposes'. 'Sure,' shrugged Gen. The room was already crowded. Her sister was leaning against a disposal bin for used needles. Her mother was next to her at the desk. I was sitting on the examining table, swinging my legs.

There was a palpable silence now. None of us were able to keep up that forced banter, the lighthearted small talk diverting our attention from the looming destiny of diagnosis. Gen's mother picked nervously at her fingernails. Gen stared directly ahead, brave, stoic, beautiful. Her blue eyes were very clear. The sequins on her jumper winked beneath the fluorescent light.

In a spectacular case of failing to read the mood of a room, the student doctor thought now might be as good a time as any to break the ice.

'Sooooo,' he opened with. 'What's the deali-o here today? What are we in for?'

We all looked to Gen. This had to be her call. How much she wanted to tell him, the details.

'I'm waiting to get some results,' she said finally. 'I've had some . . . tests.'

'Right,' the student doctor replied, nodding seriously. Adopting the 'I'm here to listen' face he had no doubt pictured himself wearing in future years when he was a highly paid GP with a four-year waiting list and a mistress named Conchita.

'We've been waiting about two hours out in the foyer,' Gen's sister explained, adding in a shaky, impatient voice, 'It's been fairly brutal.'

She was referring of course to that infinite stretch of time we had simmered in unspoken frustration, looking at the mere amount of steps between knowing and not knowing, the difference between carrying on with the rest of our day unencumbered or stepping into a whole new world of catheters and radiation. We had watched at least seven people go in before us, in varying degrees of poor health. We had envied them. At least they knew what they were dealing with. At least they had earth beneath their feet.

If this was a sign that our party may have been in a slightly fragile emotional state, the student doctor failed to notice it. He ploughed onward, sensing a misguided opportunity to bond with a room full of women.

'Oh boy, don't tell me about *waiting*!' he said with comradely eye rolling. 'The other night my girlfriend and I waited ninety minutes for a table at Mamasita. You know that restaurant in the city? They offered to give us a seat at the bar, but I'm like, "No way, we want a table." I mean, the food was amazing, don't get me wrong. But ninety minutes? An absolute joke.'

More silence. I wondered if his man-of-the-people routine would carry on if the news was bad and Gen was given three months to live.

'You think a *death sentence* is rough?' he would say, interrupting the oncologist's grim diagnosis with a wry chuckle. 'One time I had an overdue DVD at Blockbuster and was fined *eighty-seven dollars*. Oh man, was that a shitty day. I had to pay it off in instalments!'

When the oncologist finally entered the room at a brisk clip, waving his manila folder about like a baton, things were finally and instantly set on an even keel. He cut to the chase, telling Gen she most certainly had breast cancer and that it had spread to her lymph nodes and they would be performing a mastectomy within the following week.

The news was of course terrible, though I sensed most of us were doing everything we could not to look at the ashen face of Mr 'You think that's bad' over the other side of the room as he realised the moronic depths of his faux pas.

I still think about that student doctor from time to time. I very much hope he's been run over by a bus.

In a rush, more men in suits and ties entered the room, taking Gen behind a mysterious curtain and poking at her and murmuring reassuringly. As I held her mother's hand, I heard the booming voice of her surgeon cutting through.

'I wouldn't worry about this at all,' he said with confidence. 'We'll just get in there, take it out, and move on. That's always been my motto with surgery—Keep It Silly, Stupid!'

The silence behind the curtain was suddenly deafening. The surgeon cleared his throat.

'I mean—Keep It Simple, Stupid! That's my motto. Not the other one. That was . . . that was a mistake.'

This was deeply comforting. The man in charge of Gen's mastectomy couldn't even get his surgery motto straight. If things continued in a similar vein she'd be prepped for the operation by Pauly Shore and wheeled in by the cast of *Let the Blood Run Free*.

We filed out of the room in a sombre mood, not looking each other in the eye, wondering what to do or say next. Gen announced she was going to the toilet and, for want of anything better to do, her mother and sister went too. I was hovering in the hallway outside, slightly stunned, waiting for them to finish, when music started playing over the PA and everyone in the hospital paused and stood to attention.

It was the Last Post.

It was Remembrance Day.

We were at this very moment supposed to be observing a

minute's silence and reflecting upon the blood that had been spilt during Australia's wars. Gen had just been told she had breast cancer and was going to lose part of her body. And she was in the toilet. It was so absurd I couldn't help myself. I started laughing. I laughed in sadness and shock and grief for her breast. Breast we forget. A man who had dragged himself to a respectful standing position from a wheelchair glared at me. It grew worse when I heard Gen's infectious snort from inside the ladies toilet, followed by the sacrilegious sound of a flush. Her laughter set me off laughing even harder. The invisible thread of hysteria linked us through the concrete walls. We were in a restaurant again, thumping the table, shrieking, helpless, disturbing fellow patrons. Each paroxysm sending the other one off on another wave of collapse.

The diagnosis had shifted us into free-fall now, a completely unknown realm. The poor taste jokes we had always made about racism and JonBenet Ramsay took on a breathless, fuck-you-world edge.

It wasn't my first experience with breast cancer. Years before, my father's sister had developed the disease and battled on valiantly for what seemed to be a long while. I had experienced her demise with a cool detachment characteristic of self-absorbed teenagers. I knew nothing of the process of disease and acceptance. She had died slowly on the New South Wales coast, a hundred years outside of my orbit physically and emotionally. All I remembered of her now was a bird-like smile peeping out of oversized pillows. To my abject shame thoughts of her death stirred no real feeling outside of vague curiosity and a duty to share a morbid medical fact with new GPs. Is there a history of, yes I suppose so, you see my father's sister . . .

She had been a grownup. Cancer was for grownups. Gen was not a grownup. Gen was determinedly frozen in her rock 'n' roll twenties. She would join me in illicit bloody marys on Wednesday mornings after some sordid evening spent screaming abuse at *Big Brother* contestants. We went on roller-coasters together. We sat naked in the Japanese bathhouse in Collingwood, dangling our legs in the steaming, clear water and emitting helpless cackles as we compared the prowess or lack thereof of boys we had once loved.

The night before her operation we all got shitfaced in Gabi's kitchen, planning a variety of comedy wigs Gen could showcase once she was in the depths of chemo. Her favourite was a Rastafarian beret with accompanying dreadlocks. She was desperate to wear it mostly so she'd have a legitimate chance to tell the number one joke in her terrible joke repertoire. (Q: What did the Rastafarian say when the marijuana ran out? A: 'Who put this shit music on, mon?') Gabi's three-year-old daughter Delilah wouldn't sleep, insisting on lying on a beanbag on the floor listening to 'How Deep is Your Love' on repeat. She called it 'the quiet Bee Gees song'. As we poured endless wines and the jokes grew darker—one fairly poor taste routine involving how Gen was going to manipulate the Make-A-Wish foundation so Russell Brand would be forced to swing by the hospital and have sex with her—the brothers Gibb kept singing, on and on, in easy-listening tones.

When I arrived in the hospital foyer the next day Gen was already there, waiting and grinning. 'Mastecto-ME!' she shouted at full volume. Passersby within earshot, some dense with illness and wheeling IV units out onto Royal Parade for a covert cigarette, turned with startled expressions. She was standing triumphantly, one hand on her hip, the other in the air. She looked more like somebody about to be presented with a washer-dryer set and holiday to Hamilton Island than a young woman with cancer, hours away from having her right breast removed. I have never loved her more than at that very moment.

We followed a complex path to yet another waiting room where we were told to make ourselves comfortable on the plastic seats—another unceasing drag, made briefly lively when a young Albino man wearing a leather jacket and moodily fingering a crucifix decided to sit with us and fix us all with penetrating stares. He looked like an extra from *Children of the Corn* with a side career in Norwegian Satanism.

Somehow, he became an important comic figure in the surgery process. We imagined with whispers that he would be sitting next to Gen every time she woke up from a major anaesthetic, or went in for treatment, or arrived home after a long day being dissected by oncologists. We even created a voice for him, pitched somewhere between Vlad the Impaler and the chef from *The Muppet Show*.

As we killed time inventing further elaborate scenarios (Gen's sister had him tucking her into bed at night and singing Metallica's 'Enter Sandman' as she slept), a commercial for medical reality show *RPA* came on the waiting room television. 'Denise is battling cancer and fighting for her life,' the voice-over artist said in chocolatey, concerned tones. 'Tune in on Thursday night to see if she pulls through.'

There was a long pause as everyone in the waiting room fell silent. A lady nearby in a headscarf started crying into her handkerchief.

'Well, that was tasteful,' said Gen drily. 'Hope I'm still alive on Thursday so I don't miss it.'

The operation was a success and our friend Fluffy visited and took a photo of a weary-looking Gen on her iPhone for all of us waiting anxiously at home. In the picture she had tubes up her nose. She was also smiling like a prom queen and throwing the V sign. When she called people to tell them about the daily sponge baths she was receiving she seemed unable to stop herself also yelling 'SPRING BREAK' down the phone and making loud and sexy comments about the nurses.

Gen's brush with cancer took us all to dark places in our heads and we struggled to understand how it fit in the chaos of our lives. A few of our friends pitched in for a week or so to paint and repair her rundown warehouse apartment. ('You could have thought of a less dramatic way to get your apartment fixed,' I said to her, watching the working bee in action.) Other friends drank and smoked harder, as though panicked and picking up the slack. I was being pushed to meet a deadline and I snapped at my editor. 'For fuck's sake,' I heard myself saying. 'One of my best friends just had a mastectomy and I'm not in the right headspace.' It felt as though

I was making up an excuse impossible to argue with, using Gen's illness as another in a long line of 'I don't want to meet my deadline' justifications. Even speaking aloud of what she'd been through for my own purposes made me guilty and confused.

'You know what I would hate most about having breast cancer?' our friend Dan said one day suddenly, with no small amount of viciousness. 'All that fucking *pink*.'

There was a week or so after the mastectomy where the air in Melbourne seemed to go blessedly still again. Gen returned home, did her stretchy arm exercises as required and tried to gross us all out by oversharing details about fluid drainage. We chipped in and bought her an iPad, engraving one of her favourite words on the back. When she turned it over and saw that it said 'forevz' she shrieked so loud the tap-dancing school next door to her apartment fell temporarily silent.

'I have decided I am going to just walk around with a t-shirt that says "thank you" on it to save me having to say it EVERY FIVE MINUTES,' she wrote enthusiastically in a group email, 'as I am having my mind blown by the generosity and love that is being showered upon me.'

We were in a positive state of mind when we returned to the hospital for the mastectomy results. I tore off a number for the African drumming workshop and handed it to Gen and solemnly informed her that her Albino heavy metal husband was looking forward very much to sharing a djembe with her.

'And my vagina,' she said. 'He can beat out a funky little drum and bass rhythm on my vagina.'

We were waved through immediately, no waiting around, like celebrities at a premiere, and assumed our regular positions in the room. Our favourite oncologist—a man with lurid purple socks and a ready smile—entered with pleasantries about how nice it was to see Gen looking so well. 'I feel well,' she said, and meant it. About five minutes after that he told her the cancer had moved to four spots in her bones 'which of course we're unfortunately unable to treat'.

With a faint but distinguishable breath, the air in Melbourne started to ripple again.

'Things were already shitty,' I said to Gabi on the phone later that night. 'And then he went and said that with the awful timing after telling her how *well* she was looking and everything suddenly got really, really *super* shitty.' As her friends we had become instantly versed in the dialogue of cancer, only weeks before referring to it carelessly as 'that Delta Goodrem thing'. Christopher Hitchens wrote in *Vanity Fair* about the disease 'having a language of its own—a lingua franca that manages to be both dull and difficult and that contains names like ondansetron, for anti-nausea medication'. We talked effortlessly now about internal mammary nodes and learnt how to pronounce the word 'metastatic' without stumbling. Gen had been taken—Hitchens again—'from the country of the well across the stark frontier that marks off the land of malady'.

We were talked through her options. She could throw herself into chemo—'aggressive, with the hair fallout and the drugs and the what-not,' according to her obscenely cheery oncologist—or instead try a course of hormone therapy. Gen considered this. To fill the space of our overwhelmed silence, her doctor made some small talk, asking her if she was going to vote Greens in the upcoming state election.

'Will that affect the treatment?' I asked him.

He stared at me.

'I mean, if she votes conservative will you get rid of the cancer quicker? Because we're willing to negotiate. Within reason.'

He looked at us for a moment. Saw Gen trying not to smile. He forced a laugh.

'No, no,' he said. 'It's just that . . . well, not a lot of doctors vote Green. As you might imagine.'

'Fine then, I'll vote Liberal,' Gen said. 'Now fix my fucking cancer.'

She decided to go with hormone treatment, after days of agonising eeny-meeny where we pored over the benefits and hindrances of every option. In the weeks leading up to her first session she decided to celebrate the fact she was keeping her hair by booking into a variety of different hairdressers, all of whom fucked up her mane in a variety of ways.

'I look like a puppy who is clearly just for Christmas,' she texted me with an accompanying photograph of a hideous bubble perm.

The treatment itself was merciless, involving an injection to shut down her ovaries and enforce menopause on her blooming thirty-six-year-old body. She had to also suffer an hour-long drip to begin 'managing' the bone cancer. Through it all she found the time to torment us with a new and interesting catchphrase.

'Can you get me a cup of tea?' she would ask from the couch. 'I've suffered enough.'

The 'I've suffered enough' line carried her through arguments over what we were going to watch on a DVD night (*Russell Brand Live* won repeatedly: 'Please can't we watch Russell one more time? I've suffered enough'), what we were going to eat for dinner ('Oh come on, let's just get Thai. I've suffered enough') and what we would listen to on the car stereo ('What are you talking about? The new Jebediah single is amazing. You *have* to say you like it, I've suffered enough').

Our group of mates held its annual 'Shit Kringle' dinner, where we attempted to top each other by gifting the worst presents possible. Booky brought a life-sized cardboard cut-out of Robert Pattinson. Sam brought a five-dollar Brashs voucher, a record store that went into receivership in 1998. I brought a single ticket to see lowbrow American comedian Rob Schneider live. When it was Gen's turn to hand over her present, she was already laughing so hard she could barely hold her hand straight. She drew Hotman's name and he opened it with trepidation. It was an ashtray, shaped like a boob, with an accompanying pamphlet on how to cope living with breast cancer. The milk-curdle laugh struck up again. We were helpless. We banged the table. 'I'm off my tit!' she shrieked loudly.

The texts I got from her when she was in hospital should be preserved and displayed in a museum. 'They are playing the Dire Straits "Walk Of Life" in the hospital waiting room,' read one. Another: 'Musical update! Chemo ward is now piping "Stayin' Alive" through their radio PA system. Their taste and sophistication is boundless. Got to run, my Albino husband is here and wants to give me an enema.'

We continued to torment her oncologist, who was mystified by my constant appearance at Gen's appointments and would make vague, coy references to the fact that we might have been enjoying a secret life as lesbian partners.

'Have you two known each other . . . long?' he would ask, doing everything in his power not to tip a leery wink in our direction. Through the mist of treatment options and CT scans and mindless answers about what side effects would occur when ('It's different for everybody . . . we really can't say' was a sentence we would rather stab someone in the face than hear again) we kept grasping for the clarity of absurdity. When we were solemnly told a byproduct of Gen's hormone therapy would be 'a dry vagina' it was all we could do not to fall onto the floor of the surgery in schoolgirl hysterics. We felt ten years old again, staring directly ahead at the wall, trying not to catch each other's eye lest the façade of demure adulthood collapse.

He said 'dry vagina', I could sense us both thinking, in scandalised, adolescent tones. Just the term was enough to set us off. We were tickled by the thought of being seen as lesbian life partners. Our love for each other could not be bound by conventional terms. In the lift, safe from the disapproving eyes of people who daren't laugh in a cancer clinic, I acted out for Gen's benefit my role as her brittle lover.

'Well, I've not noticed much dryness in the vagina *myself*,' I told the imaginary breast care nurse. 'But Genevieve does keep a pump pack of lubricant by the bed for special occasions and birthdays.'

This journey we were on was not without its pain. We were aware, all of us, at every moment, of what this meant, the unfunny clang of mortality, the fear of silence. There were times when we'd be sitting and watching Delilah playing and without warning all the energy would be sucked out of the room and I wanted more than anything just to lie down and start weeping and never stop. The injections and the nausea and the mood swings and the back pain, none of it was remotely amusing and there were days when Gen just disappeared off the radar, wouldn't reply to texts, wouldn't answer emails.

'I was having a bad day,' she would explain with shrugs when asked about her lack of communication and we'd leave it at that, respecting the private moments she needed to howl at the moon and shake her fist at the sky and curse her stupid fucking dumb fucking unfunny lot.

We took her to yoga classes and Chinese herbalists and sat with her on sober nights when everyone would have otherwise murdered a glass of wine to numb the bad feelings. We ached for her when she shut down and we wished sometimes that it had all happened to us instead, the whole damned thing, so that she could just go on playing guitar and making bad puns and being adorably obnoxious on her Saturday night radio show happily free of troubles. But it hadn't worked out that way. Cancer chose Gen, and as an addendum it had chosen us. We may not have been able to duck out of its revolting clutches but by fuck we were going to tackle it on our own terms.

Gen continues her treatment even now as I write this. Monthly rounds of hormone therapy, waiting to see how long it keeps the cancer at bay, if she'll eventually have to submit to the hateful, pedestrian rituals of chemo and lose her vigour and her freedom to indulge in shitty haircuts. More appointments with oncologists, nobody telling us it's going to be okay, this is just a passing phase, wait 'til I tell the guys at HQ you thought it was cancer. And through it all we will continue to crack wise, and make tasteless jokes about dry vaginas and 'keeping abreast' of the situation, and Albino Norwegian death metal cancer husbands singing us to sleep. In the face of this enormous, malevolent cloud, how else would we cope? We don't know any other way. This is a funny cancer story because Gen is the funniest person I know. And this is how she chooses her story to be told. Forevz.

• • •

Here I am. Immortalised in paperback. My fifteen minutes of fame are here and sadly, it's because of the Darth Vader of disease: cancer. I would have much rather achieved it through the newspaper headline 'Russell Brand leaves Katy Perry for mystery Aussie', but alas destiny, in it's infinite nincompoopery, has decided to be an utter bitch arse.

Stop. Cancer time.

My wonderful father, who is fighting his own cancer battle, told me of a cartoon drawing he remembered seeing of an eagle swooping to capture its prey, and a mouse, knowing that it was about to become brunch, standing there defiantly giving the hungry eagle the finger. This is how I feel about my cancer. I am going to be that mouse and stick my finger up at it at every turn. Of course, there are the frighteningly dark times. I am scared. I am angry. I am shocked. But I am ferociously loved.

My strong, beloved family and my unbelievably giving, incredible, loving group of friends have acted as a collective net, and any time I have been even close to tumbling from an emotional sky rise, they have all been there manoeuvring the net into position to catch me wherever I may fall on any given day. I think that the laughter between us has made the intolerable mildly tolerable, and there is music in that.

I would like it pointed out, however, that although I am quite fond of the Rasta wig, I am not afraid of being bald. I could make a nice living covering Sinead O'Connor's early works, or as Tony Abbott's testicles. I hear he is in need of some.

I am anxious having my story 'up in lights' via this book, but it's really the only way I would want this nightmare to be recorded. Although 'in song' would be nice. Are you feeling me, Beyonce?

Now, ladies, do me a favour and get your baps checked.

Forevz.

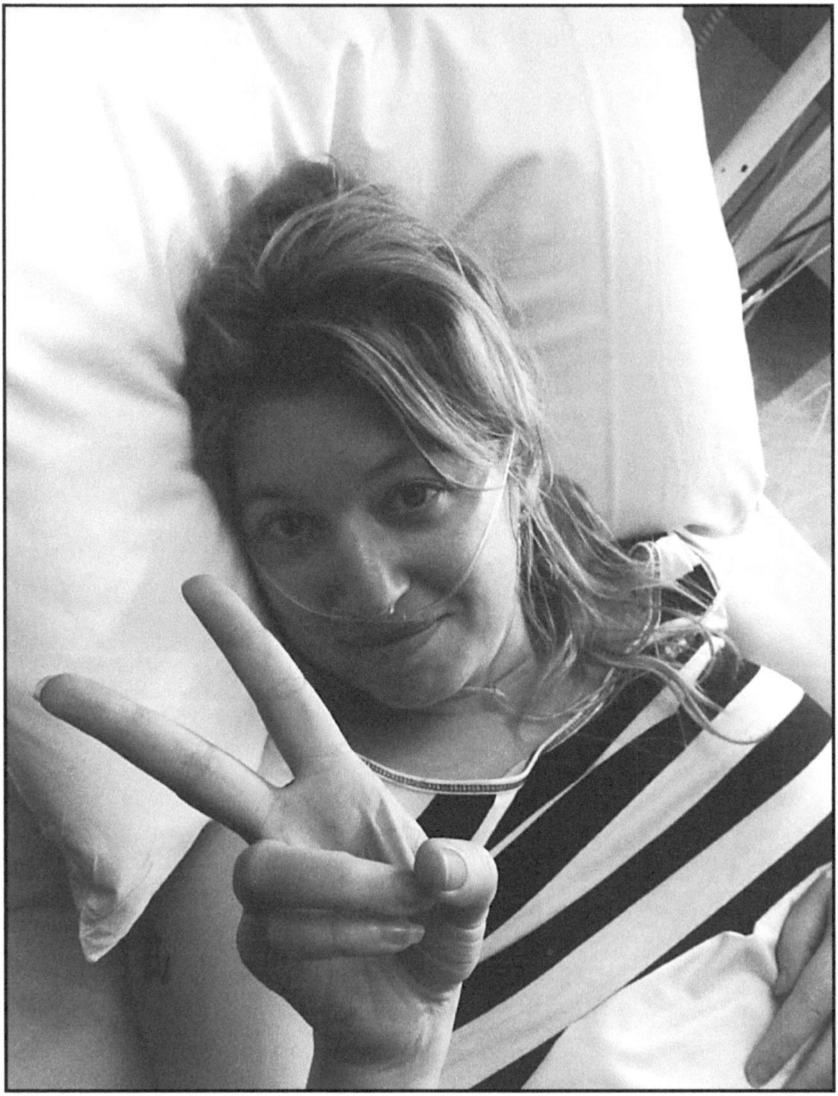

Maroon and blue

Being a Victorian you are regularly asked—by taxi drivers, by distant relatives, by umbrella-toting strangers in the street—which football team you support. It is just one of those questions that arises when you live in a certain town, an unspoken commitment to participating in the communal way of life. More often than not awkward silences follow when I am forced to admit that I don't actually support anybody. In my home state, public admission of not following a football team is tantamount to standing up on a church pew and stripping down to reveal a peek-a-boo baby doll lingerie set and the words SATAN IS SEXY carved into your lower abdomen. Australian Rules Football is so much a part of the Victorian way of life that it creeps into conversations about other, completely unrelated matters, like parking fines or major surgery.

Memo Australian Labor Party, wrote one newspaper correspondent during a recent state election campaign, *please can I be on your secret database?* The subtext could read: 'Says would rather be tied down and forced to watch continuous replays of the Collingwood grand final win than ever vote for us.'

My lack of football team is not due to some misguided snootery regarding arts funding or rapey 'any hole's a goal' players, but because in 1996 my heart got broke so bad by football that I cried for days and refused to eat. Football has the power to do that sometimes—cut you off at the knees and leave you bereft. Grown men stagger out of the MCG, weeping openly all the way to Richmond station. Wiping runny noses on Driza-Bone sleeves, they comfort each other with comradely sniffs and a rough, jostling understanding. In most cases it's the men who weep, while the women just get stony and cold. Riding the Swan Street trams, they wear the haggard faces of survivors.

When my mother and father first started dating, they attended a football game together. Being amateur theatre actors at the time, they needed a break from all the community puppet shows and hemp workshops they usually attended, and were probably congratulating themselves on retaining a link to their gauche suburban past, as arty types often do when paying to watch competitive sport. They were standing in the outer, a part of the ground usually reserved for violent men recently escaped from prison or AA. The outer doesn't really exist any more, which is a grand pity as watching a game from deep within its confines in the 1980s was an experience akin to running ashore at Gallipoli with Chopper Reed for an all-you-can-smoke meth sale. I once stood in the outer during a Richmond/Fitzroy clash and heard an obese man with a vivid coldsore hurl abuse at a nearby umpire.

'Hey Umpy!' he shouted commandingly. 'I been up your mum and she give me AIDS.'

At the time, this fairly evocative comment caused a brief but reverent silence as nearby onlookers contemplated its brutally impressive nature. Someone in the distance may have applauded. This was the outer—a no-man's land of racist insults, poor personal hygiene and the occasional jolly stabbing. It was legal to smoke in the outer. People stank of piss and stale beer and dagwood dogs. At Collingwood games whenever a supporter would yell 'COME ON THE PIES' some wag in the outer inevitably followed it up with 'Fark, and I thought it was just tomato sauce!'

When during those early days of courtship my father escorted his intended through the crowd of leering wharfies in duffle coats trying to surreptitiously look down her dress, he was fretting somewhat. My mother was a nice girl from Glen Waverly who enjoyed musical theatre and the odd game of netball. He feared it would only take one call of 'PICK THE FUCKING PIGSKIN UP YOU FUCKING FAGGOT' or 'SOMEONE TELL THESE CUNTS THERE'S A FUCKING GAME ON' to make her turn very pink in the cheeks and inform him in a rather tight and small voice that she'd quite like to be taken home now thank you and to please not bother calling again. I think it was about fifteen minutes into the game that a poor umpiring decision was made close to the boundary line, at which point my mother propelled herself to the fence, hoisted herself up to eye level with both little gloved hands, and screamed at full volume 'UMPIRE YOU FUCKING WHITE MAGGOT WHAT THE FUCK DO YOU CALL THAT THEN' and my father sighed happily and decided then and there that this was indeed the woman he was going to spend the rest of his life with.

My mother went to Fitzroy games while heavily pregnant, a time during which I am told other mothers decorate nurseries and apply lanolin to their bosoms and pat the Dulux sheepdog or other such gaily maternal activities. She would pace up and down the stands, pausing occasionally to kick out at passing children or hot-dog sellers. If Fitzroy were falling behind in the scores she would shout firstly at the game, then directly into my father's face. His long, thin frame would be swaddled in an enormous sheepskin coat, as though to cushion the brunt of her fury.

'WHAT THE FUCK ARE THEY DOING OUT THERE, ALAN?' my mother would bellow, running her hands over her baby bump in an agitated fashion. 'THIS IS A FUCKING SHAME, NOT A FUCKING GAME.'

In utero I soaked up her demon song and emerged from the womb inextricably devoted to the Fitzroy Football Club. It ran through my veins.

Fitzroy were always the joke, the patsy, the fat kid up the back of the bus who wore dental headgear and a Sugar Ray t-shirt and referred to his parents' car as 'the vroom vroom machine'. Tell a group of strangers that you supported Fitzroy and you were openly mocked, often to the point of physical violence. Following Fitzroy was the equivalent of wetting your pants at speech night and then having to perform 'Hakuna Matata' from *The Lion King* in ensuing squelchy torment. They hadn't won a premiership in so long there were club bumper stickers that implored hopefully 'Let's roar like 1944'.

My family was of course completely obsessed. While the leisure activities of other families revolved around cheery greeting-card bonding-type affairs such as Monopoly or It's a Knockout, ours centered utterly on the club. We went to what was known as the 'Ins and Outs Night' which, despite its vaguely pornographic name, was less about standing around cheering as Barbara Windsor took on all comers and more guessing which players would be picked in the team for the weekend's game. We went to training, where we'd stand in the freezing cold watching thirty sweating men running around frantically in circles and jumping over orange witches hats. As a child I would dutifully bake a chocolate cake for these sessions, wanting to reach out and nurture in some way. The players would hold a slice in their meaty paws like a delicate little flower, mumbling thankyous and regarding me with no small amount of curiosity.

Saturdays were game day. Hour-long drives to VFL Park or Whitten Oval were fairly common, the relentless tedium of the traffic only relieved by endless games of 'Name That Show Tune'. Sundays were sacred. We'd spread out the newspapers and hold Hardy family round-table post-mortems on who had played well and who had let us down, physically and emotionally.

'Richard Osborne was fucking wasted on the back line,' my mother would lament as she sipped her Earl Grey and we would all nod glum assent into our muesli mix.

I had a recurring dream where I would play in the forward pocket, like Bernie 'Superboot' Quinlan, and every time the opposition tried to return the ball to play I would interfere, manipulating my way into yet another goal, another triumph. I would lead Fitzroy to another victory single-handedly. My dreams allowed for no reasonable efforts on behalf of my opponents. In my subconscious, I was king.

Before I hit puberty I was allowed in the Fitzroy changing rooms, likely due to the fact that I used to hide my long hair up under the Commonwealth Bank cap I inexplicably wore everywhere and had about as much bosom as a Cruskit. Some geriatric trainer with a whistle around his neck and a tired expression would wave me in, presumably too exhausted/drunk/glaucoma-stricken to notice that I was a girl, and there I'd be, darting about among legs and shorts in the hallowed surrounds.

They really used to work the trainers hard in those days. They were like wizened little gnomes in tracksuit pants and windbreakers. Ancient ex-athletes, they'd spend half the game feverishly trying to keep up with the players—who either completely ignored them or accidentally elbowed them in the face during a moment of intense play—and the other half standing on the boundary line gasping for air and occasionally vomiting blood. I loved them, mostly because of their aforementioned lax security work and the fact that they occasionally let me carry the used mouthguards around in a little bucket.

There were naked men everywhere in the rooms, a fact that didn't daunt me in the slightest. I guess I was so used to seeing my father strolling naked around our house the idea of a penis parade of VFL players wasn't too bothersome. I would march up to nude twentysomethings as they towelled themselves off, holding out my autograph book and blithely ignoring the dangling manhood between their legs.

'Excuse me, Mickey,' I'd chirp, unfazed. 'Could you please sign my book?'

They'd sign it, unsettled by the sexless little pixieboy in the tiny dufflecoat gliding its way around the changing rooms at eye level with their genitals, and suddenly feeling the awkwardness of their nudity, as though I was a serpent offering them a shiny apple.

'Here y'go, mate,' Ross Lyon would say, scribbling his autograph with a flourish and giving my hat a friendly pat as he shoved me in the opposite direction. 'Stay in school eh?'

Fitzroy footballers in the 1980s were golden, brawny, glorious. There were the Osborne brothers—cocky, glamorous Richard and his shy, acne-scarred older brother, Graham. Enthusiastic, puppyish Duane Rowe. Toothsomely mysterious Gary Pert. They moved as a pack, all fleshy arrogance and pride. They slapped each other's arses and spat on the grass.

Tim Pekin was twenty years old when I first spotted him loping around the team, all stick arms and milky-spindle legs, with a terribly inconvenient fringe that fell over one eye whenever he found his way near the ball. My parents christened him 'The Poet' as he looked like he belonged at a writing desk, penning lengthy soliloquies for wealthy dowagers with a quill, rather than sprinting around Kardinia Park covered in mud or standing miserably in the rain at Junction Oval waiting for David Strooper to kick a torpedo his way. He wore a guernsey with the number 24 on it and I thought he was utterly perfect.

I was the first kid ever to wear his number on my back. I loudly insisted to all who would listen that he was my new favourite, needling my parents to purchase the iron-on transfers '2' and '4' to attach to the back of my official VFL merch Fitzroy Cubs jumper. They duly complied, privately and disproportionately amused by my somewhat eccentric choice of heart-throb. I pasted over old pictures of Corey Haim with black and white photographs of Tim sitting on a bench with a towel over his head. At night I would talk to the pictures as though they were alive.

I saw him naked plenty of times, sneaking up on him in the change rooms and playfully squirting water on his exposed buttocks or just sitting next to his locker and staring silently and innocently at him while he rushed to get dressed. I used to force my way into the weights training room at Junction Oval and stand by admiringly counting as he did his reps. He was baffled by my sudden devotion, and was ribbed mercilessly by his teammates.

'Peeks, your missus is here,' they'd snigger, flicking him in the testicles with wet towels and gesturing over to where I stood in the doorway, oblivious to anybody else in the room. I would write down topics of conversation in advance ('You know, you were really outplayed by Michael Tuck last Saturday. I'm only saying that to be constructive') and follow him from the physio's office to the car park, where I would grin adoringly into the window of his Barina until he politely locked the car doors and drove away, being careful not to run over my foot.

We would circle warily around each other during my patented Thursday night chocolate cake handouts—he gawkily uncertain of how to handle a determinedly devoted pre-pubescent, me in my numbered jumper, plotting and planning the perfect marriage proposal (should I mention the age difference or just gloss over it as though it wasn't an issue?). Tim was a horrendously shy Colac boy who wore stonewash jeans with pleats in the front, raised a Catholic with umpteen brothers and sisters. I regularly invited him over to our house for dinner, pushing insistently every time he affably sidestepped my requests with friendly chuckles.

'Oh, that's . . . that's sweet,' he would murmur, desperately trying to make eye contact with somebody across the room to come and save him.

I fixated upon the idea of dinners and wouldn't let it drop. I invited everybody. Michael Gale, Paul Roos, Gary Keane. Suddenly there was a new addition to our family's already busy football-obsessed week: Wednesday night dinners. My parents would cook up enormous platters of tortellini and spaghetti that would be inhaled in a matter of minutes by these bullish man-mountains. At first everybody was very shy. Our dining room resembled an odd sort of country barn dance, with three or four players crammed over one side of the table staring demurely into their laps, and my family on the other side attempting to coax them into conversation. After half an hour or so somebody would break rank and the room would exhale and talk would turn to sport and politics and music. And pasta. The players always liked to talk about pasta.

Tim Pekin finally came to one of these dinners. At first he was painfully bashful, and our overt attentions seemed to cause him distress. But then he came to another, and another, more regularly over time, until eventually his absence was a more notable thing than his presence. He got to know the layout of our house and would roam its perimeters more and more comfortably, running his long fingers over book spines and resting his drink on top of the piano in moments of quiet reflection while around him everybody chatted amiably. I followed him from room to room.

After my mother requested more Saturday afternoon white space in which to scream like Hasil Adkins in a voodoo froth and throw her boiling thermos at the opposition players, I was allowed to roam freely around the footy grounds unsupervised. To a child, this was heaven. I took up with a couple of broad-shouldered, smiling sisters named Cath and Jo and the three of us would duck and weave through the crowds, picking up half-eaten buckets of hot chips and trying to skeeze loose change from sentimental drunks. It was because of Cath and Jo that I was eventually inducted into the Fitzroy cheersquad, a motley collection of vocal bogans who gathered around the end of the ground behind the goal sticks and waved flags whenever Fitzroy kicked a rare goal. The cheersquad demographic ranged from three-year-old girls with earrings and bubble perms to hoarse middle-aged men sucking back durries. While the distant interstate code of rugby had rows of taut eighteen-year-old dames in butt-grazing skirts shaking little pom-poms and high kicking with excited squeals, Fitzroy had toothless slags and sporadic applause.

It was exciting being a part of something that was simultaneously so chaotic and so organised. The cheersquad would spend Tuesday nights in some freezing cold community hall, painstakingly putting together an enormous crepe paper banner celebrating Fitzroy's achievements of the previous week, all while eating Chicken Crimpies and drinking litre bottles of Solo. On game day we'd troop out onto the field and unroll our precious burden on the wet oval, shivering in the cold, and on some secret signal stagger into packs at either side of the banner and raise it up for the rest of the ground to admire. Moments later, the team would run out of the rooms and run through it, tearing it to shreds—after which point we would carefully pack up all the torn scraps into garbage bags and retire to our regular position behind the goals, knowing that we'd been a part of a special moment. It was all very thrilling.

These banners were enormous. Some weeks they'd feature

a cartoon lion, snarling menacingly at the opposition. Other weeks they'd go for a solid message of congratulations along the lines of WELL DONE GRANT LAWRIE 150 GAMES. On the ground, even when crammed into a pack holding up one side of these enormous totems, my face in a random armpit, I'd still try to catch Tim Pekin's eye as he ran onto the field. I was for the most part ignored.

As I grew into my skin and became an irksome teenage runaway, keeping my parents awake at night with a persistent habit of slipping out of bedroom windows and hanging out at recording studios with morally bankrupt guitarists, I distanced myself with emotional jaggedness from my increasingly distressed family, becoming more convinced that the mysterious, elusive spirit-connections between drunken strangers were the only ones worth nurturing. I stopped going to football games. My family's slavish devotion to the sport, the humiliating way they shouted from the sidelines, the overly hopeful way they attempted each week to bring us all together again in the name of the club . . . it was twee. It was a childish relic of a past from which I was eager to disassociate. When my father watched me dress for a night out, all hotpants and teetering teenage platform high heels, he would say in a hurt and hopeless tone, 'But I thought we could go to the game tomorrow.' I was cutting myself free from everything my parents loved, and the sacred, jolly ritual of football represented only a forgotten past.

Over the years, the club I had grown up with began to flounder. They won two games in two years. Ins and Outs nights became less a social gathering and more a place to mourn triumphant days of yore. My parents still determinedly attended games but left with sagging, defeated faces. Everybody looked tired and old, even the players. I was living a new life, running around town with goth girls and boys with facial piercings. I thought I was the shit. Every now and then my parents would try to make a connection and ring whatever slummy share house I was in and invite me to a game. For old times' sake. I would make somebody else answer the phone, pretend I wasn't home. When the telephone was returned to its receiver I would regale my stoned friends with embarrassing, self-deprecating stories about being in the cheersquad and turning up to training each week with my sunken little chocolate cake.

'I used to *cry* when Fitzroy lost,' I would tell the room, to howls of delight and derision. 'I used to go home and *talk to the team poster.*'

In 1996 it just got too hard for Fitzroy and they crumbled, brought to their knees by heavy debts and bad management and a footballing body intent on expanding the game to a national level, leaving no prisoners in its wake. There were murmurs of a merger with North Melbourne, then Footscray, then finally some dreadful half-arsed deal was done with Queensland team the Brisbane Bears and, just like that, one hundred and thirteen years of history was over. No matter how many fundraising nights or tin-rattling doorknocks the dyed-in-the-wool supporters devoted themselves to, Fitzroy would fold at the year's end. There was a dull sense of inevitability about it all. Fitzroy was never built to last. It was the lame dog, a sentimental family pet who everybody knew would get taken into a paddock and shot eventually.

I was dating an ex-AFL player that year, and at an awards night he publicly noted my disloyalty to the club I'd once adored.

'I'd like to thank my girlfriend for missing so many Fitzroy games to come and see me play,' he said in his speech, adding with a smirk 'though to be fair she wasn't really missing much since they haven't won a match in about seventy years.'

It stung because it was true; I'd abandoned Fitzroy just like I abandoned broken romances and broken friendships and things that were difficult and awkward and took time to fix, like my relationship with my parents. I resented the implication and what it said about my careless personality.

Fitzroy played their last ever game of AFL in Fremantle, Western Australia, at the Subiaco oval, on 1 September, 1996. My father had to work in Melbourne, but my mother decided to fly four and a half hours to mark the moment. We had only just begun speaking again after another vicious round of bruisings and name-callings, but in an offhand moment she asked if I would like to come and in an offhand moment I said yes. I bought a plane ticket and we sat together uncomfortably, existing in that emotional limbo parents must suffer when a child has slipped from their discipline and grasp. She had long ago accepted that I would never come home again, and seemed determined to let this trip pass without incident or recrimination. She offered me a Fantail and we sucked in comradely silence.

Once in Western Australia we behaved like tourists. We went to the old Fremantle gaol and inhaled its bloody history. We had a beer and lunch on the water. We talked benignly about the climate and the passing trade, never really acknowledging aloud why it is we were there and what the end of the team meant to us personally.

The game was a disaster—of course, of course. Fitzroy were never a chance to win, not even with some big dumb sentimental stroke of luck involving all of Fremantle's players succumbing to severe food poisoning and being suddenly unable to stand up straight or function. They fumbled and sloped their way across the oval, missing opportunities, dropping marks, kicking the ball out of bounds on the full as though they'd recently suffered a serious stroke. They looked sorry for themselves and everyone in the crowd and clearly wanted it all to be over. The handful of supporters who had made the trip across clapped politely with heavy hearts. It was unclear who was hurting the worst.

When the siren eventually signalled the game's coming to a merciful end, my mother and I turned to each other and we were both weeping. There was an unspoken shared heartbreak, an overwhelming cavalcade of memory—of falling in love in the outer, tending to a blossoming pregnancy, agitating with the cheersquad, trotting around obediently after broad-shouldered icons. I watched the team shuffle down the race into the rooms, heads lowered, full of shame and disappointment and a dark, confusing grief.

My childhood shuffled off with them. My family rituals shuffled off with them. When they had all left the ground, trainers trudging behind, I heard something click shut in my heart.

At that moment I felt my mother reach across and take my hand.

People made a lot of noise about Fitzroy's euthanasia at first. Shook their heads and muttered about 'the death of the game' and how stripping local football of its dignity was the beginning of the end. How there was no more heart in football. Corporate greed had taken over. Some drifted across with guilty expressions to Brisbane and quietly bought memberships, attending games when they could and trying to muster up the enthusiasm to follow a newer, flashier team that had essentially chewed up their little dreg of a team and spat out the remains in fleshy gobs.

A small but vocal group of supporters refused to say die, setting up a Fitzroy Football Club website and meeting regularly to discuss options for the future. They no longer had a team to follow. There were no games to attend. They were simply a club of members with an AGM and a photocopied newsletter. They were rudderless, a theatre without a play. They met in a church hall at first, then a function room, then downgraded to the odd beer garden as fewer and fewer people attended, feeling foolish at attempting to keep the dream alive.

In 2007 I penned a piece for *The Age* about Friday night football coverage and mentioned in passing my fondness for Tim Pekin's number 24. The same day it appeared in print he emailed me, for the first time in months. I asked him if he'd read the column. He replied that he'd not seen it, adding: *It seems we have a rather intriguing way of communicating, beyond the realm of ink on trees, and for that I am grateful.* He had grown into his boyish nickname, finally encompassed the soul of a poet.

I still have my tiny jumper with the iron-on 24 peeling from its back. I still believe in football and its sweeping passions. I just can't explain why I no longer have a team. How I miss the searing memory of ritual and family. And it still exists, sort of, kind of. In a different form. Or maybe I just need it to. Like those Fitzroy supporters, meeting once a year in some dusty pub, with worn-out photographs and A4 folders full of memories.

Excerpts from this story first appeared in The Age.

Pour l'album

There is a secret unofficial age, it seems, when travel with one's family crosses over from being a unifying lesson in worldly concerns and open-mindedness, and is instead looked upon as a rather sad admission of defeat. Backpacking around Europe in a shitcan Kombi with your parents at the age of eight is life affirming and to be celebrated. Doing the same thing at the age of thirty-five is embarrassing and to be pitied. Have you not got a husband?

You escape your family by moving out of the home in which you grew up, in a wilful and pre-emptive display of misguided independence. *I can do what I want now*, you tell yourself as you stretch out on a bed fashioned from milk crates and foam cuttings, admiring your dream catcher and the stereo system you have made from a stolen Discman and a pair of speakers. *They don't own me anymore.* You ration out visits to your ex-home like an unfeeling kitchen hand from a pantomime orphanage might ration out gruel. Once a staple part of life around the noisy breakfast table you become instead an elusive figure, breezing in and out of the family house in a flurry of sorry-can't-stay excuses and pervasive hangovers. As you build your own life a necessary distance forms between you and your parents, through guilt-laden phone calls that end in petulant, regressive bursts, and your selfish inability to humanise them in any way.

'They won't mind if I cancel their wedding anniversary dinner,' you tell your friends through a fairly brutal chemical aftermath. 'They've got *things on*. They've got each *other*. They're probably just going to spend the night in front of the television watching *The Bill*.'

After a while a sense of nostalgia creeps in, like months after a break-up where you text a once-maligned ex a friendly but meaningful hello. You forget the deeply entrenched destructive patterns enmeshed in every family unit and start to see your parents as affable chums, comrades with a shared history and a secret language. They're not *really* like Debbie Reynolds and Peter Sellers. They're more like the Cosbys. You should go on holiday with them again. Nothing bad can possibly happen.

A holiday with your parents when you are a fully grown adult is an exercise in patience, ego and humiliation. No longer a free agent, lying in bed 'til 3 pm reading newspapers and drinking champagne with a naked redhead, you're now beholden to the brisk, no-nonsense schedule of two health conscious over-60s who develop a quiet but significant panic when their sense of routine is in any way compromised. You must rise when they do ('It's 6:30 am, what better time for a power walk! Here, you can borrow my intensely stupid-looking handweights'), eat what they eat ('We're on Atkins! My colon has never felt better! Look, I have a photograph of my last bowel movement!'), and sit in the back of the car trying to tune them out as they bicker over whether *Brides of Christ* was a miniseries or a novel. You are taken back to your seethingly hormonal teenage years when your parents were foolish enough to invite you with them on a trip to the States, possibly reasoning that if you were at least under their noses for the majority of the time you wouldn't be compelled to indulge in the sorts of behaviour that may result in a stint in juvie.

On that particular holiday you reward their invitation and goodwill by sneaking out of your LA hotel room and going out driving with some twenty-something college student you meet in a hamburger restaurant after insisting that your parents sit at another table on the other side of the room and pretend they've never met you before. This man may or may not be a rapist or a serial killer, you don't really bother to check his credentials before getting into his jeep and gaily taking off into the balmy Los Angeles evening. After returning miraculously unscathed and unpenetrated, you spend the remaining two months and seventeen days lurching from tourist mecca to glorious landscape with a surly expression and a faceful of Judy Blume. Hapless, hollow-eyed guardians forced for some incomprehensible reason—bribes, perhaps, or a death threat against other members of the family—to ferry shrieking infants on long-haul flights have nothing on the hellishness of travelling with a teenager.

I was five years of age when my parents had first decided I was ripe for a twelve-week overseas journey. 'It will be good for her,' they told themselves whilst performing water aerobics and protesting against Reagan and drinking Tab and whatever else it was people did for amusement in 1981. 'It will expand her mind and free her from her slightly bookish and eccentric fantasy world.' Obviously at some additional point they must also have shrieked in delighted unison, 'AND SHE CAN BEGIN HER SCRAPBOOKING CAREER' as an unbridled demonic insistence on cataloguing our journey came hand-in-hand with the plane ticket.

Scrapbooks. Scrapbooks. They seemed to be obsessed with scrapbooks. Everywhere we went, every little road trip, every beach jaunt, there my parents were, pulling out the craft scissors and the Clag, collecting postcards from hotel lobbies, plane tickets, bus tokens, used tissues. They insisted I spend at least an hour a day carefully documenting the previous twenty-four hours in a combination of layered cuttings and prose, leaving no detail un-noted, no anecdote untold.

'You can't sleep *yet*,' my mother would announce with horror as I crawled into the fold-out hotel bed, exhausted from a day of frolicking in the snow in Lucerne, or having my face garishly painted by a Dutch clown, or pretending I was Superman on the Eiffel Tower, 'you haven't done your *scrapbook*.'

They even, god help them, tried to enforce the scrapbooking regime in those later years when the merest mention of a sit-down family activity was greeted with colourfully disrespectful displays of mimed vomiting. I did as I was told, though. My teenage travel scrapbooks may have been filled with derogatory snarls such as 'Went to Centre Pompidou. Gay' or the more unintentionally apt 'Went to San Francisco. Gay', but they were still duly filled and exist to this day as a memento of the trip.

Have you ever really experienced a road trip or holiday if it's not documented in some fashion? Modern roamers utilise Flickr accounts or blogs or Facebook as a sort of show-offy collection of look-at-the-fun-time-we're-having-while-you're-at-home-indulging-in-a-little-cry-into-your-biscuit photographs. Punk cabaret artist and prolific Twitter user Amanda Palmer once bemoaned, 'It's a tragedy that my reaction to seeing something interesting is turning away to grab my camera. The first thought is that there is something beautiful happening, and the second thought is that it will be meaningless if I don't share it. Those are frightening moments. The ones when you go, "God, I've been living for everyone else."' At the very least scrapbooking is a private exercise, or it is for most people who don't get drunk with a boyfriend and demand he sit on the living room floor reliving every precious memory and superglued serviette. ('Look, and here's me accidentally touching Snoopy's testicles at Knott's Berry Farm.')

I travelled a great deal with my parents. We went to Europe and America and Adelaide. I don't know where this burning desire for me to scrapbook came from. Possibly they felt if I were bent over a creamy pair of inviting A3 pages, immersed in the task of cutting and pasting and slyly ingesting the odd bit of Clag I wouldn't keep humiliating them in public. In Ireland I had witnessed some gypsy children begging for change in a crowded market and clearly felt the practice had merit. For the remainder of that trip, whenever my parents lost sight of me they would inevitably stumble upon me moments later standing on a corner with sad eyes and an upturned palm. I begged outside the Uffizi Gallery in Florence, I begged at Universal Studios. When in mortified tones they tried to impress upon me that I couldn't just stand in public places randomly asking people for money I started drawing pictures in my notebook and attempting to sell them instead. When this activity too was inevitably forbidden, I began marching up to strangers and singing 'God Save the Queen' and requesting loose change at show's end. I was nothing if not creative, and probably could have funded an extra twelve weeks of travel if my folks hadn't been such oppressive buzz killers.

Outside of all the begging and the tireless scrapbooking, that particular trip was wonderful, what I can recall of it. We saw the Louvre and Anne Frank's house and experienced a not unlively moment where we went to visit Nana Mouskouri backstage after a concert and she sang to us. I demanded to feed the pigeons in Trafalgar Square and upon receipt of a breadcrumb bag instantly managed to explode it between my tiny hands, leading to an avian frenzy my father still refers to with a haunted expression as 'that time you were nearly killed by pigeons'.

The scrapbooking gene somehow stayed with me and as I grew older and holidayed with boyfriends I would insist we document our journeys together. My first love Christopher and I used the scrapbook of our American trip mostly to have arguments with each other ('I was being a dick and Chris threw a book at me, which smacked me in the face' read one entry of mine, while another in his hand reads: 'Hello. My name is Marieke Hardy. I am a gullible, awestruck Australian tourist. Please take all my money'). We fought the whole way up Highway 1. We fought in Hearst Castle. We fought at Disneyland. We spent Christmas Day in the high-kitsch surrounds of the Madonna Inn in San Luis Obispo watching the *Star Wars* trilogy from the comfort of a novelty bed and we fought there too. It was a volatile pairing, a bad combination of zodiac signs. Travelling together brought out the worst in us, the overtired, poisonous, insecure parts of our personalities, and we documented each and every bitter falling out. As a postscript to the scrapbook we wrote a Q and A for each other to complete, with topics like 'Favourite person on the trip?' and 'America at its most kitsch!' Under 'Moments You Wanted to Chuck in the Towel' Christopher wrote simply: 'When Marieke was being a dickhead.'

Undeterred, I kept up the tradition in later relationships.

My then husband Sime and I scrapbooked our trip to East Timor and Bali, an odd little holiday that included a musical tour he did of the Timorese jungle. I met with him over there, accompanied by armed guard, and we stayed in a hotel riddled with bullet holes and staffed by one-armed bellboys. We ate fresh calamari and drank cold white wine on one of the silent, still beaches, and looked out over an enormous ball of sunset. The air was thick and warm. The sand, a mandala beneath our toes. Sime was burnt a beautiful brown, sleepy and full of love. We had been married about a year. I scrapbooked the moment with great sentimentality.

'In the future, when I feel dreadful and things are going badly,' I wrote, slowly and carefully, 'I want to think of this moment. Of us, sitting together on this beach in Timor, full and content and madly in love. There is a chance that this may be the happiest split second of my life.'

Sime obediently reminded me of it, in later years, when we were no longer together, when I was raging with passion and pain over some other gentleman caller, when the night terrors started up again and I went for weeks without a proper sleep.

'Remember our beach in Timor. Remember the scrapbook,' he would text.

Our time in a Balinese spa on the way home to Melbourne was somehow glossed over in the scrapbook, possibly due to the abject horror we felt whenever the memory was raised. There is just one small reference to it—'Went to day sp—' reads an entry on 23 May, as though the person writing had begun trembling so violently with the recollection they were physically unable to complete the word 'spa' and had instead taken themselves off to shock therapy.

We had entered the treatment area full of shy smiles, wearing all over our faces the presumption that 'people like us' don't really go for spa treatments. We never really went for *pampering*.

The day spa was a discreet little high-design enclave next to a resort swimming pool and we were ushered in with polite nods and the universal 'right this way, Sir/Madam' gestures that day spa employees worldwide are apparently taught in a secret underground laboratory. Our treatment room was beautiful, cool mosaic tiles, two massage tables, an open-air bath surrounded by deep green palms. Every towel corner was lovingly and fastidiously triangled. The musky aroma of the ocean permeated through the burning essential 'Harmony Blend' oils, and a not abhorrent form of lilting panpipe murmured through speakers at a low level.

We had extravagantly chosen a half-day treatment that seemed to involve every form of body prodding and caressing one could imagine. Our feet were to be bathed in bowls of fragrant water and flowers, we would be stroked, simmered, covered in hot oil, towelled down, slathered in mud, and finally rubbed gently around the facial area before being left alone to sit in our open-air bath with a glass of champagne and foolish hair. Given the opulence on offer there was likely the additional option of marrying the masseuse and taking her home with us as a kindly and beaming love slave, though as idealist left-wingers we of course didn't follow this up and instead probably justified our half day of self-absorbed tending to by giving Médecins Sans Frontières a gold coin donation at the airport.

We were introduced to the two very sweet young ladies who would be taking care of us, and the four of us smiled and nodded and nodded and smiled and Sime and I made some benign, joking small talk at which we laughed too hard to compensate for the silent, blank-faced reaction from our audience, and the young ladies smiled incomprehensibly and kindly and everyone nodded again and thus time passed. Eventually we were handed a white robe and a paper shower cap and with more nodding and smiling and bowing and pointing it was suggested wordlessly that we might like to shower our filthy tourist bodies clean from the scum of cocktails and cheap hotel sex and middle class guilt we had accumulated over the past week and once we were ready to begin our treatment to let them know.

They left the room backwards with more smiling and bowing and Sime and I looked at each other with helpless, embarrassed smiles. There was nothing *comfortable* about this. Neither of us was revelling in an aura of relaxation and bliss. We felt sorry for the people who would have to touch us and we thought of our crummy, overstuffed rental house in North Fitzroy and our blocked washing machine pipes. Nobody in their right mind enters a room with gilt taps and a musical water feature and thinks 'By god, I deserve this idiotic affluence' outside of Gianni Versace and just look what happened to him.

'Well,' said Sime, trying to make the best of our blushes and regrets, 'I guess let's just shower and bung these on and try to unwind.'

The robes themselves were gargantuan, swallowing up our puny frames in soft, pillowy swathes. We resembled monks from a special monastery for dwarves. I glanced dubiously at the paper shower caps in their neat little cellophane packets and decided I'd rather not spend the rest of the treatment looking like a comatose Laverne or Shirley.

'Do you think they'd mind if we don't wear the hats?'

'Oh god no,' replied Simon. 'They'll understand. I mean, it's not as though we have *dreadlocks.*'

We sat stiffly and awkwardly on the cane chaise longues, naked beneath our robes, waiting for our new friends to return. They did, in another Moomba-esque parade of nodding and smiling, before coming to a disconcerted stop directly in front of us.

One of them pointed to the unopened shower cap packets.

'Oh yes,' I replied. 'We'd rather . . . we'd rather not wear those if that's okay with you.'

'We'd just feel . . . more comfortable without them,' Simon added helpfully, smiling and nodding to support his case.

The two lovely ladies stopped smiling for the first time since we'd met them. They turned to each other with worried frowns. We had clearly upset the program.

I glanced at Simon, who shrugged his confusion. Our masseurs consulted with each other in urgent Indonesian whispers.

'Please . . .' one of them said, holding up the packets.

They were obsessed with shower caps. I held out my hands in a gesture that seemed to say 'We're all adults here, let's just get some perspective.'

'It's just . . . not really our thing,' I stated brightly.

More urgent whispers. Things were growing more uncomfortable. There was the sense that any moment somebody unseen would press a buzzer and we'd be marched from the room in disgrace, our sunscreen-stained beachwear tossed out after us.

'Maybe we should leave,' Simon murmured worriedly.

The ladies turned to us again. Pointing to the packets once more.

'We just . . . for hygiene.'

If it was so important to them we would put on the fucking party hats.

Simon was the first to open his. I saw the blood drain from his face.

'Oh dear,' he whispered.

They were not shower caps. They were paper underpants. Disposable paper underpants that all tourists having spa treatments must wear for the sake of hygiene, modesty and the general dignity of all involved. The last ten minutes suddenly replayed themselves through my brain. How we must have looked to these nice young women, sprawled out half naked on the chaise longues, refusing to wear the underwear they had given us.

It's not really our thing, I had insisted sleazily. No, we don't 'do' underpants, ladies. And if you or the management at Ying Glory Day Spa have an issue with that we'll just take our festy genitals elsewhere to be revered in full-frontal glory.

When I told my mother what had happened, she tried to put a positive spin on it.

'At least,' she said, 'they didn't come into the room and find you wearing disposable underpants on your head.'

We tried to buy drugs on that trip. Likely it was to erase the memory of terrorising two perfectly nice day spa workers with intimations of happy ending massages. Thankfully all we ended up with was a foil wrap full of henna that we tried briefly to smoke before realising we were trying to get high with something teenage girls used to look like Tori Amos. This was years before that poor idiot Schapelle Corby misguidedly grabbed her boogie board and announced to friends, 'Ready! Anyone else got anything they want me to pack?' but even still we should have known better. It was the arrogance of the young, combined with the recklessness of a traveller. *Nobody knows us here*, the passport whispers from the safety of your travel pouch, dizzy with the power of authority and anonymity. *We can do whatever we want.*

On a trip to Thailand with another boyfriend I had spent a long night doing tequila shots with friendly prostitutes in a bar before my partner loudly and cheerily agreed to get on an undersized motorbike and meet a drug dealer to buy some speed. This was an excellent idea, two highly intoxicated and fairly pint-sized tourists parting company in a seedy area of Koh Samui while one straddled a toothless, bike riding drug mule called Yick.

'You stay here with our new frens,' my boyfriend slurred, gesturing vaguely to the beaming whores over the other side of the bar. 'I'll be *righback*.'

I found him again, seven months later and living in an ashram. He seemed content.

When I went to Europe with my last boyfriend Tim, our trip was filled with afternoon craft moments in Barcelona and Parisian bars.

'Drink your beer,' I would order him, 'and *then* we'll scrapbook.'

The scrapbooking urge had remained, but I was an adult now and holidayed with whomsoever I chose. In a necessary surge of independence I spent my twenties roaming the world with friends and lovers. I saw my parents for summer weekends or day trips. It seemed we had silently agreed to leave our family vacationing in the annals of childhood.

I was thirty when they asked me to holiday with them again. My father wanted to go on a pilgrimage to visit an indigenous community, Kalkaringi, that his father helped set up in the late 1960s.

When we set out, I was hungover after a night seeing loud rock'n'roll bands at the Rob Roy. A smear of ink on my wrist and Jägermeister remnants aching through my blood. More importantly, I was now a grown woman and would be sharing a campervan with my parents for the better part of two weeks. And I had a head like Rick James after a four-day bender. It was not an auspicious beginning.

They met me at Darwin airport, full of smiles and hugs and won't-this-be-just-like-old-times jolliness.

'Did you bring your scrapbook?' asked my mother, only half joking.

We hired a ridiculous-looking campervan, an insistence on the part of my father, the only heterosexual man I knew who actually understood and admired the term 'glamping'. The van had a television and a microwave. The only thing missing was an eight-person jacuzzi and personal butler. As my parents inspected it, my father climbed inside with a grin.

'Isn't this *fantastic*?' he said to me, clapping his hands gleefully like a dizzy chorus girl on Broadway.

The campervan salesman looked over at me with a smirk. He was wearing pleated trousers and an Akubra hat. I felt myself cringing like a humiliated teenager again, feeling his judgement. *Have you not got a husband?*

We drove from Darwin through crowded Batchelor, sleepy Pine Creek, vicious Katherine. The woman working in the local post office wore a t-shirt sporting the Australian flag with the words IF YOU DON'T LOVE IT, LEAVE plastered across it and I heard my mother and I tsk loudly at the same time. We caught each other's passive-aggressive middle-class protest and turned, suddenly and shyly, feeling the tug of the invisible umbilical cord.

In the van they entertained and humiliated me; singing Easybeats classics loudly out of the window and bombarding passersby with their intriguing range of comedy accents. The laidback people of the Territory were clearly bemused by Mr and Mrs Boy from Oz and their overgrown retarded child. When we booked into caravan parks I would find myself slinking away for time alone, burying myself in a book and silently wishing—not for the first time—that I had at least one other sibling to bear the brunt of my parents' aggressive love and companionship.

Travelling with them again brought back visceral memories. They were hands on, engaged. Everywhere we stopped they wanted to read from pamphlets and point out interesting facts and take photographs. It was like going on a roadtrip with the presenters of *The Curiosity Show*.

The first night we slept together in the van I lay awake for hours, listening to them rustle and shift and snore. Far from being of comfort, it was a lurch into quiet panic.

If they have sex, I thought, *I am definitely going to kill myself.*

At night we would eat barbecued fish and drink gin and play cards. I would sneak extra wine in order to try and overcome the discomfort of being bunk buddies with my mother and father.

'Just going for a little walk!' I would tell them, heading directly to the van park bar. I would sit in the baking heat, reading Vonnegut and drinking from face-sized glasses of syrupy warm Territory wine. By the third night I was so rolling drunk I accidentally tried to get into bed with them.

Kalkaringi was an odd place; frankly startled into life by the 40th anniversary of the Wave Hill walk-off and ensuing two-day party that we were there to partake in. Everywhere you looked there were ABC outside broadcast vans and random community groups being bussed in from neighbouring towns. Teams of teenage boys with gargantuan surly clodhoppers of shoes roamed in sullen packs. People were there to celebrate Gurindji Freedom Day, marking the famous 'handful of sand' moment immortalised in the song 'From Little Things Big Things Grow'. It was utterly impossible to be anywhere near Kalkaringi without having Paul Kelly on endless rotation in your mind, like some kind of twisted jukebox. I could hear people humming it as they went past.

My father was due to make a speech, and he was nervous. He locked himself into the campervan for an hour and we watched it wobble as he paced inside, continuously bumping into the bar fridge with a merry little explosion of, 'Oh, for fuck's sake!' My mother looked over at me.

'It means a lot to him that you're here,' she said.

I wasn't comfortable with this overt sentimentality. I ached for a drink.

'Well . . . whatever.'

'It means a lot to me too.'

I kicked at the dust like a mule.

'Your dad never came here with his father. Frank was always so emotionally distant, and Alan was incredibly independent . . . I suppose when he was growing up he found Frank slightly embarrassing.'

The thought that my father might have been embarrassed by his own parents had never crossed my mind. It was the territory of the young.

'I suppose he saw bringing you here as a sort of—reaching out, generationally. We know you're busy. It's really lovely that you took the time.'

Busy being drunk, busy drinking Jägermeister shots at the Tote. I felt suddenly and deeply ashamed of my overgrown adolescence.

There was a ceremony. People spoke about my grandfather in a way that made him sound like an important stranger. Some local kids got up and sang 'From Little Things Big Things Grow' in a shrill vibrato. Everybody clapped and fanned at flies. And then it was my father's turn.

'When my father came here, he had no spirit. He had lost his ability to tell stories. The Gurindji people and their spirit inspired him . . . and through this inspiration he found his spirit and his stories once more.'

He looked around at the silent mob of faces.

'When I was last here, I sat with Mick at the Victoria River and he told me that my father's spirit lives here, with the Gurindji. We owe so much to this place and its people. Thank you for having us here with you today.'

It was heartfelt and succinct. My mother's face was wet with tears when he returned to his seat, but I saved mine until I was safely returned to the bosom of the crowd; big dollops soaking behind my oversized sunglasses, safely hidden beneath my Stevie Nicks hat with the swooping brim. I wasn't even certain why I was crying until my dad reached over and took my hand for a reassuring squeeze.

The drive back to Darwin was infinitely more relaxed. I joined in the singalongs and tried not to hide in the back when my mother insisted we take turns in re-enacting scenes from *Bugsy Malone*. As we motored into the campervan rental yard I felt a sharp stab that this trip would be taken from me before I truly had a chance to appreciate it. I berated myself for wasting precious moments anaesthetising myself with liquor when I could have been doing cartwheels in the desert sand. As we unpacked the van I found a collection of serviettes and business cards in a small plastic bag, along with a notebook and a tube of glue.

'For the scrapbook,' my father said, when he saw me standing with it. 'We thought you might like to do it at the airport while you're waiting to board.'

I had been saddled with the responsibility once more of maintaining the memories and to be honest I wasn't exactly sure I'd been sober enough to document anything past 7 pm. I tied the neck of the bag with a knot and placed it in my luggage. We hauled everything out of the van and stood looking at it, feeling the scorch of the sun.

'I don't know about you two,' said my mother, 'but I could murder a scotch and dry.'

• • •

On travels overseas now I shun the dozy, blinking tourist routes and attempt to blend into the landscape, to immerse myself in the daily life of a town and only participate in the occasional modest begging episode or two. When fragments of memory return from that Darwin trip they are inevitably less about the magnificent landscapes and culture and more about my relationship with my parents . . . what it felt like to fall asleep in a strange van to the sounds of their breath, how they challenged me and educated me and continued to show me the world despite my best efforts to drive them crazy. And when I hunger for the detailed anecdotes, the dates, the places, the people, the francs and pennies and lire, I go directly to the scrapbook and am transported instantly to an A3 cache of perfect recognition.

Parts of this story first appeared in Sunday Life *magazine and the* A2.

The business

It's nobody's fault specifically that I was a child actor.

My parents were against the idea from the outset, and tried to discourage me by saying educational, nurturing things like, 'It's not that we don't want you to be an actor. It's just that we'd prefer you to do something more productive and fulfilling with your life, like ingesting peyote and running naked onto a busy highway.' They had both been actors themselves, and knew the emotional tumult, creative humiliation and crippling self-doubt that came hand in hand with consistently prostituting oneself out for auditions in front of unimpressed directors named JP or Cozzo. It was a difficult world, a lonely one. It was a world that destroyed upstanding human beings like Winona Ryder and John Barrymore and Gary Busey. They were naturally afraid for my long-term wellbeing.

Before I was born my father's stint as 'the Australia Post guy', had involved adorning pamphlets at post offices nationwide that provided people who may not have known any better—those awakening from a deep coma perhaps, or hairdresser to the stars Lillian Frank—with information and helpful hints on how to send parcels and aerogrammes. The 'How to Send Air Mail!' one was a particular highlight, featuring as it did my father wearing an aviator jacket and flying goggles whilst standing inside a cardboard box, scarf flying out at an angle implying great gusts. I used to study these pamphlets with intense concentration, digging them out of the shoeboxes he'd stuffed them into years earlier, forgetting them along with his unfulfilled dreams of ever being the next Henri Szeps.

My father is on a pamphlet, I would marvel. *I am without question the luckiest kid alive.*

A VHS showreel of his earlier performances was later brought out to humiliate him at some party or other, introducing friends and family to a whole new chapter of his acting career. He had cut his teeth on the stage in children's panto, and then spent a miserable few years repeatedly saying yes to the corporate cock suckingness of commercials and a humiliating handful of forgettable background guest roles. That footage of my father in a bowler hat and false moustache exists for posterity while Peter Cook and Dudley Moore's seminal sketch comedy series *Not Only . . . But Also* was erased by the BBC and left to die is, I'm aware, brutally unfair and an all too grim reminder about the futility of human existence as a whole.

The best of my father's commercials was for Bristol Paints. He played an over-eager junior salesman wearing a velour v-neck sweater over a white skivvy, and flared trousers so tight it's a miracle he was eventually able to work up enough semen to create a child. His long-suffering manager was, if memory serves, a man with the all-purpose boss name 'Mr Weatherbee' or somesuch, and whose sole job was to look ham-fistedly fed up while my father comically knocked over precariously stacked pyramids of paint tins. Dad also did a television advertisement for a popular '70s wine label that involved him pacing a bottle shop wondering how to match the foods he was serving his fussy girlfriend with the vast and confusing array of alcohol on offer.

'Rita doesn't like seafood,' he bemoaned to the portly shopkeeper, who rolled his eyes and nodded sympathetically at the general idiocy of the gentler sex. They agreed eventually on a three-dollar bottle of sticky port or something equally reflux-inducing.

I grew up telling people 'my father's an actor' which ironically set off the same sorts of pitying tsks and frowns of disapproval he had experienced thirty years previous when informing passersby that 'my father's a Communist'. I didn't know that theatre folk were to be looked down upon and treated as tiresome jesters who had never grown up; gypsy spirits with a lax attitude to finance and sexual morality. One teacher at school weighed me compulsively, as though possessed with a secret knowledge that my parents were blowing precious grocery money on frivolous purchases like glittery costumes and trapezes.

'You've lost point three of a kilo,' she would say accusingly, picturing the delight on my father's face as he selfishly took delivery of a shiny new pair of maracas while I wasted away in my bedroom. The other children in my class looked on without comprehension. I was weighed more than anybody in my grade. One day she weighed me three times.

When I was born my father was working in the script department on a popular war soap called *The Sullivans*—a show since described as 'like *Neighbours*, but with bombs and Hitler'. Unable to rid himself completely of the acting bug that had infested him as a teenager, he shamelessly wrote himself a modest part in the series. This was to be a common occurrence with my father, and if one day you're short of amusing things to do you can search his name as a writer or producer or script editor on IMDB and find almost without exception that whatever shows he worked on in a behind the scenes role, somewhere his name will also appear in the cast list. It's hard not to admire his naked ambition. I imagine him sitting in production meetings, script in hand, broad smile across his face.

'You know who would be *perfect* for this role?' I picture him saying in a hopeful, sing-song voice while his colleagues shifted uncomfortably and wondered just how long it would take before management grew wise and fired him. He played a returned soldier in *The Sullivans*, a priest in riverboat series *All The Rivers Run*, and someone known memorably as 'Customer 1' in *Homicide*. In overlit, overacted police drama *Cop Shop* he either played a character called Streaker or an *actual* streaker, I have been too afraid to ascertain which exactly.

Coincidentally, the first acting job I ever had involved me

getting naked, which set the lowbrow tone for the remainder of my drawn out and tawdry career in front of the camera. To my eternal shame I allowed myself to be stripped down and placed on a rubber bath mat, appearing alongside my smiling mother, who at that time was sporting the haircut of the day, a sharp, glossy bob and fringe made popular by daffy *Hey Hey It's Saturday* co-host Jacki MacDonald. My job was to look inherently delighted by the fact that with the assistance of scientifically proven grip tests I was enjoying bath time without all the bothersome business of slipping over and knocking myself unconscious on the soap dish. I believe I acquitted myself with aplomb. I was, I think, fifteen months old.

It seems unlikely that I was nagging my parents for an agent prior to the bath mat commercial. At that point it was all I could do to pronounce the word 'kaka' and not wet the bed. Which does seem to suggest that they are partly to blame for my crossing the line from insufferable family showoff to professional actor. 'One bath mat ad won't hurt,' my mother must have said, ironing her bob into its sleek, rigid helmet. 'And it's not like she'll remember being naked in front of an entire camera crew. If anything, we're doing her a favour by getting her out of the house.'

Child actors are, on the whole, abhorrent little creatures. Brittle dwarfish adults with forced, eager-to-please smiles and the sort of complicated maze of eating disorders usually found on the set of Bret Michaels' *Rock of Love*. They are forced into constant adult company at an age where they should instead be curiously sticking their fingers into each other's pants behind the shelter shed or eating rocks, and accordingly grow intolerably precocious. They tell jokes they don't fully understand, they become sexualised long before it's healthy and occasionally at Christmas they'll utilise that weird politician-style double-hand handshake, unnerving grandparents with their robotic manners and cold, dead eyes.

I became one, seamlessly. I took to it like Wilson Tuckey to an unhinged racist epithet, and graduated from bath mats to tap shoes. Once my parents had accepted that I wouldn't be swayed from my bloodthirsty lust for stardom, they were reluctantly and dutifully supportive. They permitted me to go to ballet school even though I showed all the co-ordination skills of an epileptic duck. They sent me backstage flowers on 'performance days'; interminable afternoons where one hundred and fifty girls under the age of eleven wearing leotards flung themselves about beneath a cloud of toxic hairspray to songs like Cliff Richard's 'Summer Holiday' or the less conventional Toto Coelo classic 'I Eat Cannibals'. I showed no talent in any particular area—jazz, classical, modern; I was determinedly dreadful at all—yet persisted gamely.

'I want to be a star . . . like Little Orphan Annie, or Astro Boy,' I told disturbed relatives at family gatherings.

In *All the Rivers Run* I got my wish, playing a delightful street urchin, running amok on the streets of Echuca in voluminous skirts. My parents were producing the series and I bothered them incessantly until they allowed me on set for the afternoon to elbow my way in front of the camera.

I have since spent my entire life dodging accusations of nepotism. Clearly I didn't do myself any favours as a child by forcing my way onto everything with a Hardy name in the credits. In children's series *The Henderson Kids* (Season 1) I can be seen in the background of a scene protesting outside a logging mill with my mother. I am six years old. And yes, my never-say-die father gave himself a role in that show too. He was a corrupt high school teacher who stole precious excursion money and spent a not unmoving confessional scene wringing his hands and stroking his chin in a way that suggested deep remorse. You should see it, not a dry beard in the house.

They were obviously paranoid about the association too. For the Henderson Kids 2 I was made to audition three times because my father was so worried that casting me would damage both his reputation—what was left of it after giving himself so many plum acting roles in his own productions—and my innocence. Eventually I got the role and spent the subsequent ten months playing Sally Marshall, pigtailed pesky neighbour to Tam and Steve Henderson. Wherever there were scrapes, you could be sure I was in 'em! And so forth. I was a reasonably terrible actor, but even more mortifyingly I had yet to grow into my cumbersome peg teeth and subsequently had the sort of lisp people would shield themselves from with wet weather gear, as though my mouth was an out-of-control car driving through a puddle of words.

Imagine those excruciating, sullen years of your pubescence, between the ages of about ten and fifteen when you gracelessly straddled the bridge of childhood and adolescence. Nobody survives this period unscathed. Overnight you morph from lithe, fresh-faced, eager-to-learn wee little boundling, to chunky, poor-postured, stringy-haired slattern. Your brows grow together, you get angry smears of acne, you've not yet learned how to hide the fact your untameable hair grows brittle and upwards, like a Steelo pad. When you look back at photographs of yourself from that time—always somehow sullenly mid-present opening at Christmas, cheeks flaming red, oversized t-shirt to hide your lumpy, misshapen frame—you see the adult you will one day become, trapped in the body of Alf. Imagine now that you had spent that particular period devotedly ensuring that every agonising moment of that interminable process was captured on film and later broadcast on national television. And that at any moment of grownup reprieve years later where you want to start congratulating yourself for being a not abhorrent human being, someone will dig out the Aquavac commercial where you are parading around in front of the camera sporting high-waisted boardshorts and a cowlick.

It's there forever for me, like a time-lapse camera of puberty, like a flick book any stranger can thumb through to watch my boobies grow in fast motion. All the bad haircuts, the ravaged skin from poorly applied makeup, the period where my face was so full and pudding-like it appeared as though I was orally smuggling a pair of hackey sacks. The speech impediments, the costumes you can tell I'm agonisingly self-conscious in, the thickly knit monobrow. If my parents had really wanted to dissuade me from a career as an adolescent actor they need only have said, 'Listen, you're welcome to do it—but we're going to compile a "best of" reel for your twenty-first birthday and it will feature you wearing too-tight leggings and a polo neck and rescuing a wombat and anyone who sees it will never want to have sex with you again.'

In school I was monotonously in every production. Carey Baptist Grammar did *Man of La Mancha* in 1990, a musical theatre show about a man losing his mind and chasing windmills which seems a torturously apt analogy for the tumult of adolescence. There are really only three main roles—Don Quixote, Sancho Panza and Aldonza—and outside of a few speaking parts for priests and jolly inn-keepers the majority of minor roles are either town drunks or whores. There's nothing like being in a high school production where fifteen teenage girls are cast as a chorus of prostitutes. All those hormones on stage, intermingling like an oversexed gumbo. The *Herald Sun* letters page would have a field day.

The year after that we did *My Fair Lady*. They cast two Elizas, one who could sing and one who could act. I was the acting one. Given my Saturday mornings at the National Theatre Drama School (inhale, collect air in diaphragm, look meaningfully to back of room) I KNEW HOW TO PROJECT (exhale), so they had little choice but to allow me the role. Unfortunately, every time I opened my mouth to sing children in the front row wept. It's widely understood that in the previews a heavily pregnant woman in the stalls went into labour during my rendition of 'I Could Have Danced All Night'. Rebecca Leitch was the singing Eliza, and later in life she went on to have a long and successful career in opera. We swapped roles on alternating nights, star to chorus, star to chorus. I'd watch her slay them with 'Wouldn't It Be Loverly' in her rich alto while I overacted as a florist wench and fashioned character traits that would make me stand out, like an alarming tic of the eyelid or a cartoonish limp.

My parents gave me the ritual card and flowers on opening night. My mother had written in the card: 'Chookas for the run, Miss Eliza Doolittle. And remember: P. E. E!' This stood for 'Projection! Eyes! Energy!'—three essential parts of an actor's journey, though I can see how a passerby catching a glimpse of the card may have simply assumed I had bladder issues and even as a teenager needed to be reminded by my mother to urinate before taking the stage. My parents were there at every performance, never wavering in their support, always driving me home with constructive criticism along the lines of, 'Well yes, I can see how a racegoer at Ascot might get so excited they spontaneously vomit into a pot plant, but I'm not sure it's the best thing to pull focus from Rebecca like that when she's trying her hardest to hold a high note.'

In *A Midsummer Night's Dream* I played Flute—a man who dresses up as a lady, then changes back to a man again, which confused pretty much the entirety of Year 5—and in the next year was shunted to the role of Phebe the shepherdess in *As You Like It*, while the far more beautiful and talented Elissa Elliott took the part of Rosalind. Phebe was a thankless role, requiring mostly that I race about swishing my petticoats through a forest made of cardboard trees painted by the Year 7 art class, the community service chain gang of high school. My love interest, Silvius, was a very nice boy named Ashley Warmbrand who stood at least a head shorter than me. 'Sweet Phebe, do not scorn me; do not, Phebe,' he would squeak in an unbroken quaver, staring determinedly at my chest. I spent the majority of my time glaring hatefully at Elissa Elliott from the back of the stage and years later experienced an entirely mean-spirited pang of satisfaction when I saw her on television advertising fungal creams.

My stage career took me to *Eeny Meeny Miney Mo*, an amateur theatre piece that boasted as being 'written, staged, directed and performed totally by the Agora Players!!!' which in theatre speak means 'we couldn't afford the rights to a real play so just made up our own!!!' The cast age ranged from fifteen to forty, and the show was a mish-mash of sketches about 'relationships' written mostly by a young cast who had experienced very little outside of holding hands with James Grant on a playground swing. There was one particularly intense sketch called 'Feelings' which involved us all pairing off in the dark and writhing around while somebody in the wings played panpipe. This was my favourite part of the show because I was partnered with an intensely handsome hippy actor in his twenties named Sim and we pressed up against each other with a breathy, unscripted urgency. I looked forward to 'Feelings' with an unhealthy intensity. I think one night I may have actually cried when the sketch finished.

I moved out of home at sixteen and started doing idiotic things like shaving my head and wearing nightgowns over baggy old men's suit pants. It was the '90s. A sweep of adolescent girls were doing the same thing, aping Courtney Love's kinderwhore style and pretending with sneers and middle-finger salutes that they knew how to play guitar. I stopped being offered roles as a sweet, lisping girl next door and started auditioning for parts as mental patients and homeless teenagers. On *Stingers*, an undercover police drama starring Peter Phelps as a man who very much liked rolling across car bonnets in a butch fashion and yelling things like PUT THE GODDAMNED GUN DOWN, I played a pregnant junkie who held up a service station with *The Secret Life of Us* star Samuel Johnson. The makeup department was instructed to put traces of white powder around our nostrils 'for authenticity'. On *Raw FM* I was a lesbian stripper who wore nothing but ruffled underpants, feathers and a jaunty waistcoat. On *A Country Practice* I played a demented character named Yesterday Hubble—spawning the immortal line of dialogue, 'I thought I told you that yesterday, Yesterday'—and stalked an otherwise respectable doctor who climbed out of a hospital window to escape my unhinged lust. Yesterday Hubble ended up running away with a man in a trenchcoat who kept lizards as pets.

On *The Bob Morrison Show*—a series starring a talking dog, and another to which my father was attached so I mustn't say anything too unkind or sarcastic—I was a gothic psychopath, making one whole episode's worth of life a misery for Elissa 'just three easy applications and you'll say goodbye to fungus for life!' Elliott, who had irritatingly and to my mind unfairly again landed a leading role over me. I relished delivering acerbic comic put downs to her character's face like, 'Is that your real hair colour, or do you use bleach?' (Hush, my father is reading) and probably put more bile and viciousness into the character than was originally intended. I even tried to adlib a few pertinent barbs related to my inner turmoil regarding all the parts she'd rudely stolen from me but I'm fairly certain my aside, 'And in what sort of shit-crazy universe would Rosalind wear a push-up bra and Esprit bodysuit anyway?' ended up on the cutting room floor.

Without much success I competed for roles against the infinitely more successful Melissa George (*Home and Away*), Radha Mitchell (*Sugar and Spice*), and Rebecca Smart (*The Shiralee*). Rejection after rejection began to crack my once impenetrable confidence. The inevitable downward trajectory my parents had suffered was making its inherited presence felt.

And then, of course, there was *Neighbours*. *Neighbours*, a series that has been on Australian television for exactly eight hundred and seventy three years—Doctor Karl Kennedy began life as an Indigenous dot painting on a cave wall, true story—chronicling the lives and loves of the residents of an unassuming yet dangerously lively Erinsborough court. Between good neighbours becoming good friends, as the theme song insistently informed us every weekday, there were weddings, car crashes, pregnancies, and the odd explosion that mysteriously occurred directly when ratings seemed to be taking a leisurely dive. Every Australian actor in the history of time has played a role in *Neighbours* at some point, however small. Russell Crowe played bad boy Kenny Larkin. Ben Mendelsohn played somebody forgettably named Warren Murphy. Greg Fleet—one of the finest and most interesting stand-up comedians in the country—breezed through his role of Dave Summers, a character famous only for running down one of the show's most popular cast members, Daphne Clarke, and killing her in a splatter of PG-rated blood and gore, which is to say a single delicate arc of tomato sauce against the windscreen.

On *Neighbours* I played a small-time crook named Rhonda Brumby, living proof that ten years after Russell Crowe's appearance the writers were still fairly creatively challenged when it came to naming characters. Rhonda Brumby was fresh out of 'juvie' and full of the sort of cartoonish bad girl swagger usually seen on cockney skanks parading around the set of *EastEnders* employing rhyming slang instead of real words. I actually got to say the line, 'Don't sweat it, boss—I've got the old bag wrapped around my little finger' and nod menacingly. I was running a stolen goods racket out of Marlene's antique shop (Ramsay Street was a badlands in those days) and eventually sent packing after a hair-pulling scrag fight with a character called Bianca Zanotti. The inmates of Wentworth Detention Centre had nothing on our tussle. We slapped at each other, shrilly squealing things like 'Oh yeah? Well how do you like this, moll?' until I tumbled to the carpet, humbled and subdued and ready to be packed back to reform school where I would presumably Turn Over a New Leaf on the off chance my agent could negotiate a returning role.

I had sat around the *Neighbours* green room with the other actors, who were convinced they'd be able to throw together a markedly improved script in a pinch and had no issue whatsoever with undermining the tireless plotting work of their story department. I had rolled my eyes in a comradely fashion over the clunky dialogue and D-grade storylines, and was thus mortified when a month or so later I landed a job as a storyliner and sat in the writer's room listening to the script department make equally poisonous fun of the actors. It was an all out faction war, with the major casualty being the show itself. Tauntingly, the actors would change all-important lines whilst on set, breezily throwing away plot points on the spur of the moment in order to slot in private jokes. In retaliation, the storyliners would conjure up increasingly absurd and humiliating scenarios for the actors to play out. The end result was a show full of characters wearing ludicrous things like fishing waders and lampshades whilst trading adlibs and making no sense whatsoever.

The production company responsible for *Neighbours* decided in a burst of inspiration to install the writing department out at the studio for one day a week, so the actors could have access and discuss ideas for stories and character arcs. This should by all means have been a seamless exchange and friendly, bridge-mending process and probably would have been if the majority of actors weren't so blindly ignorant of the scripting method itself. They'd come to us, one by one, with poorly hidden agendas about getting kissing scenes with cast sexpot Kimberly Davies ('I just think my character would really *connect* with Annalise as a *person*') or wildly inappropriate storylines about heroin addiction and AIDS. Actors always wanted to play heroin addicts or AIDS victims, simply so they got the chance to rub red makeup under their eyes and deliver dialogue in dramatic, award-winning gasps. One of the very pretty male leads came to see us for a long discussion about where his character was going and how ready he was for some truly meaty storylines.

'I just . . . I want a chance to stretch myself, you know? Really—go to some dark places,' he said to us, gazing through the glossy, floppy fringe currently sending thousands of *TV Week* readers into gusset-dampening swoons.

We took him at his word and spent the next week plotting a story that was, for *Neighbours* circa 1996, relatively dark. We gave him cancer. It was television cancer, yes, which meant that it would probably never be properly named or treated and that it would only last for about eight weeks before everybody moved on to worrying about Harold Bishop's upcoming tuba recital, but for an actor on a 6 pm soap it was at least a chance to show off some good 'staring death in the face' performing. Characters with cancer get to cry, punch paper thin walls in fits of anguish, and scream things like 'Tell it to me straight, Doctor Karl. How long have I got?' before collapsing in a dramatic faint. If he wanted dark places, this story had 'Silver Logie' written all over it.

The next time we all met out at Channel Ten, we pitched the story to him. He listened to the whole thing impassively before chuckling quietly to himself as though there had been a dreadful misunderstanding yet we as simpleton writer folk weren't to know any better.

'I didn't say,' he explained slowly, just to make sure we were taking it all in, 'that I wanted to *cut my hair.*'

As he left the room he glanced at me, annoyed and hurt that as a fellow actor I hadn't helped him out in some way; understood that when he'd said 'dark places' he'd actually meant kissing scenes with Kimberly Davies that went for longer than three minutes. There was the sense that as somebody who had worked alongside the cast I should have been better equipped to fly the flag for them behind enemy lines.

I had seen the looks on their faces as they entered and noticed me there at the table, sitting with the much maligned script department and plotting the next degrading episode in their career.

Traitor, I could feel Lou Carpenter thinking. *Scab.*

Suck it up, Lou, I thought meanly in return, unwilling to be tarnished. *You should hear our nickname for you when the producers leave the room.*

It was the first time I had felt a real chasm between myself and the acting world and I felt a stab of regret, as though I may have been making a dreadful mistake and leaving my people behind. Every time I sensed myself veering away from the punishing treadmill of auditions and headshots I made a desperate grab for the nearest role available, no matter how demeaning. I accepted walk-on parts as feral protestors, voice-overs for Cadbury's. I even spent five fairly gruesome evenings covered in fake blood screaming hysterically at the aftermath of a car crash for a road safety commercial about dangerous driving. My character was a daffy passenger who distracted her chum to the point where our vehicle ploughed into another car and killed its driver, leaving a crying baby motherless. Our tagline: Concentrate or Kill.

The whole world of film sets was intensely familiar and difficult to leave. Sedentary, conventional childhoods involving tennis lessons or catching the bus to school were things other, more well-adjusted friends from normal families had experienced. For months at a stretch I had lived on location, away from home. Colac, Echuca, Broken Hill. I had grown up too fast. I had lived in hotel rooms with scant regard for the discipline of schoolwork, surrounded by adults at all times. I had drunken nights with crewmembers and been stung by the insidious politics of the production office. On location, there was a reckless 'school camp' feel—everybody went to the pub after wrap and cheated on their spouses. What happens on tour, etcetera. It set an unhealthy foundation for relationships for years to come, and that transient sense of believing that you can inhabit and abandon a family within a matter of months.

Then the roles began to fall away. And over time I stopped chasing them with that panicked feeling of missing out. I no longer went to castings. I stopped reading scripts. My loyal agent held on for a valiant number of years before she realised that I hadn't updated my headshot since I was seventeen and there was utterly no point sending a twenty-five-year-old along for the role of pre-teen runaway Amber 'Giggles' McCoy.

Yet an acting past haunts you in the way no other shameful previous professions do. Loose on a wild weekend in Surfers Paradise, a topless barmaid in a strip joint stopped me as I walked past.

'Excuse me,' she said, little brown boobies jiggling beneath the disco lights. 'Weren't you on *The Henderson Kids*?'

It wasn't as bad as the blindly offensive opener 'Didn't you use to be . . .' but was awkward regardless. At least she had a reference point. For a long time people would stand in front of me, trying to figure out where they knew me from. 'You went to Deepdene Primary School, right?' they would ask, certain that they knew me from childhood, a familiar face amongst the sandwich triangles and asphalt. 'No . . .' I would say politely, affecting a mirroring puzzled look, and implying with murmurs we'd figure it out together one day in the near future and marvel at how we'd ever managed to let such an obvious fact slip our minds.

Twenty-five years after the shoot, the cast and crew of *The Henderson Kids* held a reunion party. Everybody gathered together on a freezing Melbourne Sunday afternoon to compare stomachs and breeding capacities, in that way adults do. There were all the former child actors of the cast, jostling noisily in a bar, looking tired, looking smeared with drink, looking, if you squinted, a little like the fresh-faced stars of a 1986 television show who had been filled with air and then deflated again, like a packed away bouncing castle. Some were still acting. Some presented *Play School*. Some were addicted to heroin. We exchanged comradely smiles and sympathetic stories of the dire state of the Australian film and television industry, or at least the parts of it that no longer employed us. Behind us, on a projector screen, were images of our more successful and wholesome past. Freckled, buck-toothed, ringleted, these kidlets from promotional shots in happier days rotated slowly like relics from a happier world.

I felt for those still in the game. They seemed lost. You could see them trying not to look at the younger, better-looking versions of themselves as they talked up their walk-on role in the MTC production of *Uncle Vanya*, or three-week guest spot on *Packed to the Rafters*. 'I just did a corporate video with Iain Hewitson,' said one haggard gentleman, who had played a member of feisty onscreen BMX gang the Brown Street Boys. I felt suddenly grateful for that chasm between my old life as an actor and the one I led now, doling out poisonous barbs and settling debts with people like Elissa Elliott and Peter Phelps from the privacy of my own home. With writing there is an inherent freedom, the ability to be your own boss and keep working when nobody is watching. More importantly you can write in your underpants. You can act in your underpants too, though I'm fairly certain my days of acting in underpants—my own or anybody else's—are over. Perhaps I'm still just waiting for that phone call from my agent, the one telling me the perfect role has finally arrived and I'm to drop everything at once and claw my way back to D-grade stardom.

'You'd be crazy not to take it,' she will say. 'It's a heroin addict with AIDS. You were born to play this part, Marieke. It's time, time to return to the fold. Your people need you.'

BARBARA GANGE
MANAGEMENT
Marieke Hardy
BG
M

A gentleman guest

My life felt fairly beyond repair when it was suggested to me that Dan move in.

I was in a bad way. I cried pretty much every time I spoke to someone on the phone. I would take the dog for a walk and try to hold back tears through the streets of Brunswick, in big gulping graceless hiccups. I would start crying at the Video Ezy on Lygon Street when they wouldn't allow me to rent *Four Lions* because I had accumulated too many fines. The workers there eventually started looking sorry for me every time I walked through the door, knowing that without fail within about twelve minutes I would start crying again. One of them, a boy with an eight gauge lobe piercing, began saying 'here she comes' under his breath when I entered. I left every time filled with utter despair. I couldn't even muster the dignity to blow my nose.

'Perhaps we can come over tonight,' my mother would say, worried that I was going to spend the rest of the evening listening to Captain Beefheart records and jauntily slitting my wrists in the bath. 'We could bake a cake.'

I was thirty-four years old. I did not want my parents driving from East Hawthorn to Brunswick to help me *bake a cake*.

'I'll be fine,' I said, through a bout of noisy, un-fine tears. 'I'm just going to . . . sit and look at a candle or something and wait until I go to sleep.'

I had briefly considered killing myself but spent four hours trying to figure out who would feed the dog while I was lying on the bathroom floor choking on bloodied ribbons of my own puke and in that time lost my enthusiasm for the idea. And something a similarly harrowed companion had once said to me kept rolling through my head like the sea.

'I could never commit suicide,' he whispered in the dark. 'Because then I would never find out who or what was around the corner. And I am by nature a very curious person.'

A broken heart was responsible for it all of course, the fucker, the worst kind of internal tsunami. I had until then considered myself immune to the platitudinous nature of heartbreak, and was not known for being outwardly emotional. When something bad happened I would study it at arm's length with a puzzled and autistic expression, as though pain and hurt were simply a jagged little Rubik's Cube, waiting to be solved. If people cried in front of me I got nervous like Rain Man and started pacing. Then suddenly it swept through, heartbreak in its big black wave, obliterating everything in its path. I had overnight packed my bags and joined the community of the emotionally stranded. Worse, I had become a spontaneous weeper.

Nowhere in Brunswick was safe from my crying jags. I imagined that the people who lived in the surrounding streets would hear tiny painful grabs of my breakdown as I walked past.

'*—verything is just shit,*' residents of Albert street caught in a passing wail of despair.

'*—ing left to live for,*' others might have been treated to as they paused and looked up from their macramé or fixie bicycle. Occasionally I would walk into La Paloma and hand them my coffee cup and just indulge in a little cry while they were making my flat white. When I started crying at the chemist, Gabi gently suggested it might be time to get a roommate.

'Maybe with someone around the house,' she said, 'you won't feel like crying as much.'

Dan had been single for a long time and would occasionally Facebook message me with glum yearnings for 'bookish girls with good vocabularies'. I would think, *Wait, that's me* and a second later remember, *But that's Dan*, which essentially put the end to any further romantic musings about the situation. We had known each other for so long, periphery visitors to our respective friendship groups, that any sexy novelty had worn off an age ago. We were kindred souls in many ways, never content with our lot, fretting about relationship commitment and never quite managing to get it right. We careened from romantic fuckup to romantic fuckup, leaving a trail of misty-eyed and pissed off ex-suitors in our wake.

He was unbelievably handsome, with a peppery quiff and Clark Kent spectacles and pointy black 1960s boots. When he sang he sounded like a cup of tea with whisky in it and he made girls stir crazy. We wrote to each other late at night, lamenting our inability to move on from previous love affairs.

I mused: 'I guess the more you realise the sparsity of choice on offer, the more you hark back to times when you were truly happy and madly in love . . . and yearn for such feelings again. It really is a twisted way to live, and makes it very difficult to move forward. I suppose there has to be an acceptance that it's very rare to love as fiercely and all-consumingly as one does in their early to mid twenties.'

He had been drifting for three months without a house and needed somewhere to settle, to sort out his head and his heart and his career. I had a spare room and an idiotic new habit of crying in Video Ezy. Our friends urged us to take the leap—it made sense, it would be good for each of us, take us out of our self-absorbed, self-pitying cocoons and project us into a world of mirthsome, fresh-faced home sharing. In their minds we would spend evenings laughing gaily over Scrabble boards, teasingly flicking tea-towels during the washing up, and emerge in a month or so as completely tolerable human beings. Dan and I moving in together was a major emotional investment on behalf of our friends. Perhaps if we were entertaining each other in the privacy of our own home we'd be less likely to bore them into tedium with tales of our disastrous love lives next time we ran into them in a bar.

The house itself was a squat old chook, unconventional by Brunswick standards. It had once existed as two adjoining apartments and since been clumsily renovated. It spread out sideways, two bathrooms, two living areas, four tiny bedrooms. One room was painted Ken Done blue. The tiny bathrooms were tiled with cheap marble. I would joke about the extended space, telling visitors 'my study is in the west wing. We keep the servants in the east.' The backyard was spectacularly overgrown with weeds, and during one Boxing Day party one of the guys from *Puppetry of the Penis* had decided on a whim to do me a favour by gathering them up and setting them on fire, which impressed the Moreland Fire Department no end when they turned up at 5 am with an industrial hose. At night you could hear the bogans at the Retreat Hotel singing along to bad country music and shouting hotly in pill-soaked ecstasy.

Dan and I planned a dinner to discuss whether moving in together was a fine idea or a recipe for disaster and were both nervous, selling ourselves as housemates like skittish dancers auditioning before a line of disapproving choreographers. 'I cook a lot. I have this great Le Chasseur pot,' he said before he'd even sat down. 'I'm in a fruit and vegetable co-op,' I countered, trying not to get guacamole all over the table. 'I get a box of organic fruit and vegetables every Thursday.' We were inadvertently entering into a game of personality one-upmanship. Impressing upon the other what easy-breezy individuals we were to live with.

'I go to the gym four times a week,' I said.

'I'm a member of a swim squad,' Dan replied.

Topics also covered during this showcase meeting involved how generous we were, how totally not passive-aggressive we were, and how much we enjoyed 'really getting things out in the open' when there was a minor domestic issue. In short, we were practically perfect people and the rest of the world would be out of their minds not to want to share a residence with us.

I hadn't had a housemate in twelve years. I'd lived alone or with partners, apart from one brief and hedonistic period living with Gabi during which time we did things like take baths together and ingest acid and spend the ensuing evening crammed in our wardrobes eating watermelon and thinking our shoes were alive. It had been unconventional, and for the most part very pleasant. I hadn't had to tip-toe around overtired circus performers, or pull dreadlocks from a blocked drain, or confront heroin addicted postal workers about stealing my beetroots. There had been petty arguments with boyfriends over fetid workboots left in the bedroom but those were usually sorted with a friendly arm-wrestle and time in bed. You couldn't sleep with housemates as a problem-solving measure, or you weren't supposed to. They were colleagues, people you nodded to politely in a corridor.

A friend years ago had lived with a pothead doctor named Raymond who one day started speaking in tongues before going apeshit and smashing everything in the house. He left in a rage, screaming that everybody in the building was a pornographer, before climbing into his car, driving to Canberra, and attempting to drive up the steps of Parliament House. My friend swore off sharing a residence with anybody ever again.

'Housemates are the devil,' he told me solemnly. 'And they will eat your soul. Live alone. Forever.'

It seemed like sound advice. But I had come to the point of looking at a new housemate like medicine. A dose of newness was a potential solution to what my mother was now referring to as 'that crying palaver'.

After we had eaten, Dan raised the topic of the public way I chose to live my life. 'All that online stuff . . . that's your business,' he said carefully. 'But if I move in here and I want to, I don't know, sleep with the entire Swedish netball team on a whim or something . . . I don't want to wake up the next day and read about it on a blog.'

I promised him no, of course not, what he did in the privacy of his bedroom and studio was his business entirely and I would wait at least three days before posting it on music discussion board Mess + Noise, just joking, his filthy netball sexing secrets would be safe with me.

There was a warm and slightly gauche hug on the doorstep and we promised to think over the pros and cons of a share house arrangement before making any firm decisions. I waved him off into the night. He blinked a few times behind his exceptional spectacles and climbed into his Tarago and drove away.

Please god, I thought. *If he moves in, don't let me get involved with him.*

If Dan and I moved in together now and hooked up we would be the living embodiment of the last two people left at the party. We had once skirted around each other in a flirtatious fashion but never done anything about it, mostly because we were probably too busy sleeping with everybody else. In particularly drunken moments he might say something suggestive in a noisy bar, or I would make some bawdy reference to us one day getting married and moving to the country. Yet the impetus to go further, to lean in for the illicit kiss, or take up the lewd, teasing suggestion of a night full of fucking and perspiration, simply wasn't there. We would throw these double entendres out to each other and then grin, foolishly, as we watched them float harmlessly to the ground.

There was a sense of familiarity with Dan. Of getting older, of acceptance, of romantic regrets. We were both difficult people to be in relationships with—vain, moody, elusive and dissatisfied. I imagined the two of us curling up together in his bedroom and looking at each other's ageing bodies with a sort of grim acceptance. *I've fucked everything else up*, we would say to each other, *so I suppose you'll have to do.*

And I didn't want to fall for Dan if he moved in. It seemed like a tiresome and predictable outcome. Like everyone would expect that and find the inevitability inherently amusing. When I told my mother I was thinking of living with him she said, 'Oh, like you could control yourself around *that* wonderful boy.' The two hopeless creatives, drawn together on a balmy summer night after cooking dinner in their underpants. Unable to resist the comfort of nearby flesh. We would be the joke, the patsies. While all of our friends lived their lives in stable partnerships, with children and mortgages, we would be the errant teenagers. Who couldn't make it work with anybody else so had settled—with shrugs, with embarrassed, knowing smiles—for each other.

There was also the misguided impetus of staying chaste for my ex-partner. When I had told him Dan might move in he had looked at me with knowing eyes. The girl who kissed that sad-eyed drummer, he would think. Like you could resist a domestic scenario with somebody like Dan. At your age. At his age. At your disgraced combined ages. I told myself that somehow I would—for once—resist the siren song of the troubadour, that I would wait for Tim, that I could just sit it out in a monk-like existence in my bedroom in Brunswick while he in turn sweated it out in our country house, trying to quit liquor, trying to pay his bills, trying to move on from me.

'Goodnight, Dan!' I would say brightly and determinedly. 'I'm going to bed now!'

I could do it. I *would* do it. I would leave him, handsome and bespectacled and smart and bookish and lonely, sitting in our living room, thinking of new songs to write and dreaming of a woman to love who wasn't me and I would be strong and close my bedroom door and not budge morally if he ever did that 3 am tentative knock and asked in a hoarse whisper if I were still awake.

Yet I knew it was the most difficult of moral tests. Your heart is broken, almost beyond repair. You know you should stay single for a while. It's time. You need to learn how to be on your own. You hope—kind of, sort of—that after some months, you and Tim will work things out, that he will realise with a start the terrible mistake he has made by walking out. What better way to challenge the boundaries of your resolve than moving an intensely attractive, creative, single and lost musician into your spare room? With any luck you will hear him singing. With any luck you will hear him having sex. With any luck you will accidentally see him naked. That shouldn't complicate your head at all.

Over our initial dinner, Dan had sensed my trepidation.

'You needn't worry,' he'd laughed nervously. 'I'm not a midnight rapist or anything.'

Still I fretted in advance, heinously. I looked at his Facebook photos for the first time in a long while and thought *what if* and *what would I do if* and berated myself for even entertaining such madness. We would be housemates, housemates in our mid-thirties with failed relationships and low self-esteem. I imagined us, in the dark, acting it all out. I had tasted it long before it was even served up.

My hope was that we would wear each other out with revolting homely behaviour before we got a chance to do anything even mildly sexy. I would hear him piss without that comforting lull of post-coital intimacy, he would see me in my writing outfit of tea-stained singlet and leggings. I wouldn't look good in the mornings. I would be a wife before I was a mistress. We would together kill off any potential. Our domestic habits would be the pesticide that protected the crops of our loins from flowering.

There was also the possibility, of course, that we would never be able to relax in this shared abode. When you live with somebody you're even slightly attracted to it's difficult to exhale, to ever truly stoop to your true potential as a low-brow swamp-dweller. It's as though you need to be on your A-game at all times on the off chance a clothes pegging session in the backyard might lead to some sort of swooping, *From Here to Eternity*-type kiss.

I imagined us getting ourselves ready in our respective bedrooms.

'Oh, good morning Dan,' I would exclaim with cheer, looking up from where I reclined casually on the couch reading the newspaper wearing a gold lamé gown and full '60s cat-eye liquid liner. 'I didn't know you were up.'

At that point I was still obsessing over Tim. When he went on three-day benders and failed to return texts I would check into our dangerously still-linked bank account and retrace his steps.

'He caught a sixteen dollar taxi in the early hours of Monday morning,' I told Gabi on the phone. 'Where do you suppose he was *going*?'

I was no worse, really, than a stalker. Without urgent intervention there would likely soon come an evening where I drove back and forth past his house in an armoured tank until somebody called the police. If Dan moved in he might be able to crash tackle me to the ground next time I went to the front door eighteen times in a row 'just to see if Tim's car is parked outside'.

The main issue was that I didn't trust myself. I'd had a revolting predilection for musicians since the age of sixteen and had dated one after another, picking them off like a game of rock 'n' roll Guess Who. When you're in your early twenties this seems like a relatively adorable character trait and you're able to pass yourself off as a kind of Kate Hudson-esque free spirit, though left untamed this sort of penchant eventually turns one into the sort of badly rouged disaster area who gamely appears at Enrique Iglesias concerts gyrating in the front row with pendulous breasts knocking gently together like an executive stress toy.

There was no real reason for it. I loved music and I couldn't play it, though this sort of logic could equally be applied to driving a manual car and performing triathlons and as far as memory serves I never dated Jacques Villeneuve or Daniel McPherson. Men who played music appealed to the wanton, self-destructive part of my psyche and I indulged it compulsively. Nothing really says 'let's get married and enjoy a long and stable future together' like watching your surly troubadour brood silently in the corner of a party for three hours before smashing a wine glass over his head and punching the stereo simply because 'the vibe was shitty'.

Most of all, though, I was scared of being alone. In my brain, I married and divorced people within seconds of meeting them. I could barely concentrate on the conversation we were having without already replaying it in more intimate surrounds, picking it apart and laughing at our self-conscious selves from the safety of bed.

'You were so *nervous*!' I pictured myself saying to this stranger, now naked and familiar and full of relief.

It was decided that Dan should move in.

He arrived one afternoon in an apologetic bedlam of boxes and guitars, and proceeded to set himself up. The blue room—my favourite in the house, my old study—suddenly had a futon mattress on the floor and highbrow-looking paintings leaning against the wall. There were already records splayed on the floor, a clock radio. It looked like a boy's room. When Dan left to get another load of his things from storage I stood in the doorway of what was now his space and looked at it for a long time.

I had no idea if he was harbouring the same concerns as me. It seemed unlikely—he felt overall more centred, less raw from heartbreak. He didn't appear at all bothered. Yet they still hung there. We had talked, often, about wishing we were married and settled with a child and a partner. Now we were living together.

In the beginning it was like a sexless marriage with awkward chuckles. I felt uncomfortable seeing Dan with wet hair, listening to him eat. It seemed intensely intimate for two people who didn't really know each other that well and when he emerged from the shower I would retreat, with blushes and stammers, to my bedroom. Unused to another presence in the house I would sometimes be startled when I walked in the front door and found him in the kitchen.

He seemed to fret about being in somebody else's space and edged around uncomfortably like a lodger. The ghost of Tim lingered. We tried to look out for each other, good Samaritans in the company of the lonely.

'I worry about you getting enough Vitamin D,' he would say, opening the door to my new study and letting the sun stream in from the backyard. When he left the house I would close it again and simmer in the murk.

And yet we found, over time, a gentle way forward.

I liked the sing-songy way he spoke to my dog. He really was an excellent cook and would lean over the stove with sweaty frowns like a proper chef. We stopped laughing nervously at each other's jokes and avoiding eye contact when we passed each other in the hallway. One day I walked into Video Ezy and paid my fines, leaving the boy with the piercing surprised. There was an almost imperceptible exhalation. I suddenly knew Dan and I would not sleep with each other. We had negotiated through the dark erotic terrain and found ourselves, on the other side of it, grinning dumbly into the sunlight.

A very nice boy with a soft beard and eyes the colour of being lost at sea asked me out on a date. For want of anything better to say I said yes. It was either that or stay at home constantly logging into Commonwealth Bank online banking and I was beginning to suspect that the latter wasn't the healthiest of nocturnal hobbies.

When I emerged from my room, wearing heels and lipstick for the first time in weeks, Dan looked up from his guitar.

'Where are you off to? You look spectacular.'

'I'm going on a date.'

He smiled, briefly, and wished me luck. I thanked him, closed the door behind me, and walked into the future.

• • •

Turfed out of my Footscray abode in early November, i embarked on a sort of managed homelessness for the summer.

I slept in all manner of posh and tawdry hotel rooms while touring my comedy apocalypse themed group across the country.

I dozed under a piano in Fitzroy during a Sri Lankan metal party, slumbered painfully upright in a chair in Warrnambool after accidentally going home with a handicapped girl and napped occasionally in my uncle's tiny studio (shed) that was so loud it seemed built on St Kilda Road rather than next to it.

I sampled couches from Coburg to Northbridge, jammed myself in the back of a Tarago (!) and snoozed in a shack on Bruny Island.

A relative's mansion in Clovelly gave me a whole week of the good life and a little indie house in Northcote gave me another.

I crashed in a rattly old student house during a

cyclone in Darwin, shared a shed loft in northern New South Wales with a large huntsman (spider) during a major flood event and begged my way occasionally into my long suffering ex-girlfriend's bed.

It sure saved me some money, and it's true initially i felt like Neal Cassady but by early March i was going mental. I didn't have the cash for my own place but kept baulking at little rooms in share houses with people i didn't know or 20-year-old fans who'd responded to my ill-conceived Facebook post.

So when Hardy sent me a message about her front room i was not entirely desperate but pretty close.

I did some checking with friends and discovered that she'd just broken up with her man Tim who i liked a lot. Although i'm single and have a fairly vivid imagination and she is smart and funny and great-looking it was really my lust for real estate that drew me to her. I wanted a room with my stuff in it with a door that closed on the world. And the only time i had slept with a flatmate before turned horribly bad as she managed to eject me from my own Elwood share mansion place and send my Kingswood to the wreckers in one cunning move (Our ecstatic semi-crazed hippie/rocker couplings were almost worth the pain but only almost).

Armed with these bittersweet memories as a kind of psychic shield i trooped off to have a vegan meet-and-greet dinner at Marieke's place.

I had a quick check of Facebook before i headed off though and there she was on my news feed re-enacting a famous '70s photograph of Derryn Hinch and playmate Allyson Best.

She was topless on a bed reading the paper.

Her breasts were truly magnificent.

Oh dear, i thought, this could be interesting . . .

I cleverly reframed the situation on the cab ride over. Now i had seen her near naked then at least the curiosity factor was gone (this evil curiosity factor has been undoing hapless flatmates since the first share house in the Garden of Eden). And at least i wasn't moving in with Derryn Hinch.

Marieke met me at the door like i was a returning soldier and showed me around. I noticed the house had a taxidermy theme and the largest living space was devoted to her dog Bob Ellis who slept on a hair-sprinkled couch under a giant painting of herself. The decor was kind of vegan semi-gothic/indie and all the blinds were pulled down.

I tend toward a kind of faux-Balinese guitar shop vibe myself but i'm nothing if not flexible.

And i didn't want to go back to that chair in Warrnambool.

The two little rooms looked just right for me and the vegan meal was radical. She cooked a big and bold style and didn't nibble nervously at her meals or cover her mouth with her hand when she ate. I liked this a lot. There were also thousands of books everywhere and not all by Bob Ellis.

I even had my own bathroom.

And as a kind of coup de grace the neighbour Bob Lakis the bouzouki-playing web designer (who could explain the meaning of life to you using only the terms 'wow' 'fark' and 'good grief') popped his head through the back fence and said (strangely enough) 'fark!'

I was sold.

I texted Tim the ex to let him know i wasn't moving in on him, so to speak, just moving in. We had both been cuckolded by the same drummer in the past and i wanted him to know i wasn't pulling the same trick on him.

He was pretty relaxed and gracious about it.

A few friends raised eyebrows but ultimately they were glad i wasn't asking for their couches anymore.

So here i am.

Resident of Brunswick and cohabitant with a blogger/writer/tv star/spin-class fanatic.

So far so good.

She is only slowly realising that when i say i'm getting up early i might not actually be out of bed till eleven (she stopped buying me morning coffees after the fourth one in a row went cold).

And so far Bob Ellis the dog hasn't been allowed to sleep in my bed.

And she busted me on the net in my room singing along to that Rebecca Black song.

But things are pretty sweet.

Last night there were ten lady writers over for dinner and hardly any room to move at all.

Awful.

Swing, swang, swung

There is a very fine episode of documentary maker Louis Theroux's *Weird Weekends* where he 'immerses' himself in the culture of swingers. Aligning himself with a couple named Gary and Margaret, he follows their preparations for a home sex party and interviews them along the way about their hopes and dreams for the evening. One particularly memorable scene involves Louis and Margaret steering an oversized shopping trolley through their local supermarket and filling it with party goods—paper plates, napkins, corn chips, watermelons, something alarmingly known as 'Vita Bone'—as they discuss who might stick what up who first once everybody had 'relaxed'. There's something inestimably sweet about discussing frottage whilst holding plastic disposable cups with cartoon balloons on them.

'I've been swinging since the '70s!' claims Margaret proudly, while in the background blissfully obese American shoppers trundle past with bulk purchases of toilet paper and Ruffles potato chips.

In another scene, Gary walks Louis through their neat, suburban house, describing which rooms will be turned into dens of iniquity on the night of the party and which will be left as 'purely domestic'. They move through the special fetish enclosure, the purpose-built multi-roomed stable Gary has built in the backyard ('This is kind of what we're known for . . . our backyard and our pool area,' he says with no small amount of pleasure) before moving inside, where Louis stumbles across a sunroom that has been filled wall to wall with stained mattresses and floral cushions. It is like a padded cell with bad manchester. There are a couple of worn throw rugs and pillows that have seen better days.

'Oh, this . . . this is our indoor group room, for group activities and multiple couples and that kinda stuff,' Gary announces to Louis's enquiry. 'We put out towels, 'cause if there's any kind of fluid, it's polite not to get the mattress wet.'

He surveys the room with a mayorly pride, adding helpfully: 'We have a lot of my relatives over at other times, and they sleep in here too.'

Swingers get an undeservedly bad reputation. They're always being portrayed on television and in the movies as oily, gap-toothed men offering up their blousy, overweight wives to anyone drunk enough to take them on, or people like Gary who counter very reasonable queries about unhygienic sex in his swimming pool with the inane defence, 'I have a very good filter!'

There is a swingers club on the way to Melbourne Airport that I enjoy pointing out to people as we pass, as though a guide on one of those 'see Melbourne's seamy underbelly in its basest form!!' personal tours. It's an old chemists' building with the windows badly painted over, and a tattered New Zealand rugby flag covering the glass of one of the upstairs rooms; an afterthought to block hangover-piercing light in a dodgy share house. There's nothing remotely startling about the place at first glance—although it is painted a lurid burgundy, not really a colour that says 'nothing to see here folks, just keep walking'—yet the discovery that behind its black front door a weekly free-for-all takes place is nothing less than thrilling. Swingers! In the neighbourhood! Somebody call the *Moreland Gazette*!

Years ago my then boyfriend and I went to Sexpo, an annual event advertised as 'Australia's Premier Sexuality and Adult Lifestyle Exhibition'. Sexpo—ironically, like most of the products it is hawking—is a far sexier idea in conversation than in reality. You imagine a kind of sexual nirvana, where healthy, attractive, open-minded couples stroll hand-in-hand around the booths, picking up diamanté vibrators and letting them glisten in the soft light as they consider purchase. In reality it is a giant industrial shed filled to the brim with a combination of curious, gawping bogans trying to talk their girlfriends into anal sex and taxi drivers searching for herbal date-rape drugs. The nervous chatter and shrill laughter ricochets off the tin ceiling and fills the room with an unbearable cacophony of mindless noise, which intermingles with the unmistakable tang of sweat and fear. Every year you talk yourself into going, imagining that *this* year will be a little bit sexy, *this* year you'll come home with an array of gingham scanties and riding whips, and every year you end up sitting silently on a tram holding a showbag full of safe sex brochures and caramel flavoured condoms and wondering just how long you can put off ever having to see another person naked again.

The year we went was no different, and after three desultory circulations around the room and one particularly unsavoury encounter with an obese man dressed as an X-rated Garfield, we were on our way out the door requiring a stiff drink and a hose down when we found something that caught our eye.

A couple in their late thirties were standing next to a booth labelled MELBOURNE'S MOST EXCLUSIVE PRIVATE SWINGERS NIGHT. The man had dyed blond hair and stiff, high-waisted jeans. He eyed us with interest as we stood in front of the booth, glancing through their advertising material and business cards. His wife was a tight little package with a broad, engaging smile and warm eyes, like a sexy primary school art teacher.

'*Soooo . . .*' She started over in our direction. 'How are you two enjoying Sexpo?'

We lied that we were enjoying it just fine. And she?

'Oh, I *love* this time of year. Meeting new people. It's like a big party!'

Her enthusiasm was hard to fault. She really did seem to be having a good time. Her eyes darted around excitedly, and we had the distinct sense she may have been waiting for someone better looking than us to come along. When her social flitting swept her off in another direction, shrieking hellos at a pair of familiar faces, the man who through polite mumbles identified himself as her husband pressed a pamphlet into our hands and disappeared after her like a crowd controller at a Britney Spears concert.

The pamphlet itself was basic, made clearly from a home office computer printer and featuring ornate purple borders, the type you might see on a year nine project about the origins of Valentine's Day. Inside were further, more detailed introductions to 'your hosts' Alan and Cara, as well as a mild description of what a night at Melbourne's most exclusive private swingers night might entail. ('Discretion assured—a safe, secure, relaxed party, where couples can explore each other in a supportive, sophisticated environment.') There was an email address and a mobile telephone number with a request not to call 'during business hours'.

We decided to contact them. Obviously we made this decision when we were drunk, two days later, when the stain of Sexpo had begun to recede. It can't have been *that* bad, we told ourselves. And they seemed like nice people. Open-minded. It couldn't hurt to find out a little more.

'We're not committing to anything,' I said to my boyfriend, topping up my enormous glass of wine. 'It's just a phone call. We're just *curious bystanders.*'

Given that we'd already exchanged face-to-face pleasantries at Sexpo it was presumed we'd be swept into Alan and Cara's sacred circle and welcomed with open arms and legs, possibly given a hero's welcome and ticker tape parade. It was not so. Getting information about their swingers party was going to be more difficult than translating the rantings of a crack-addicted Welshman. Alan and Cara demanded photographs ('Full face headshots please, no hats, masks or wigs'), money up front ('Fifty dollars per person, to be transferred into account name PLAYFUL FRIENDS PTY LTD'), and to converse with us at length on the phone before they'd even begin to impart important details. What difference our telephone personalities made at this point was anybody's guess, but we dutifully called (outside of business hours) and took turns talking to Alan, like teenage girls passing the phone between them when pranking the school heartthrob. Alan had a list of questions, mostly for me.

'Have you done this sort of thing before?' he said. 'What aspects of swinging interest you the most? Are you a sub or a dom?'

It was like a quiz in *Cosmo*'s sealed section. I felt deeply embarrassed about being put on the spot, and concerned that any wrong answer might result in a mocking bark and abrupt hang up.

'We haven't decided to commit to anything yet,' I wanted to tell Alan after every probing question. 'We're just curious bystanders.'

I guess they were just trying to ascertain that my boyfriend wouldn't turn up on his own, leeringly holding a bottle of wine and shrugging 'She got an urgent job in Tokyo and couldn't make it. Now, where's all that free pussy I've heard so much about?' which apparently was an all-too-common sin in the swinging world. Men would place photographs of themselves with a beautiful looking woman on adult websites, promising to bring their better halves along for long and involved games of Pin the Penis on the Vagina, only to duck in on the night with a shifty expression and some lame excuse about how sorry Leanne was she couldn't make it. These women never existed, they were simply a front to get erect men into couples-only parties, and Alan and Cara were doing everything in their power to prevent such a thing occurring at their private event.

'They don't want a *cock forest*, you see,' my boyfriend later informed me with a solemn expression.

I pictured a roomful of sad-looking men standing around with their erections undulating lightly in the breeze, *wisha wisha wisha*, like Enid Blyton's magic trees.

When Alan and Cara finally believed that I was a real human being and not simply an animatronic device tricked up with a lady's voice, they proffered us an invitation to their next party. It was to be held in three weeks' time, and we were emailed a list of the rules we simply *must* adhere to if we were to be allowed entry.

These rules, we saw, were strict and numerous.

Unaccompanied men will NOT be allowed entry.

Small amounts of alcohol are permitted (no red wine please!!!) but we are a DRUG-FREE event and anyone found breaching the rules will be asked to leave IMMEDIATELY.

'Why no red wine?' I asked my boyfriend.

'I don't know. It might spill on the carpet or something.'

'It might spill on the *carpet*? What about all the semen??'

There was also the matter of 'small' amounts of alcohol. In our world, 'small' meant a bottle of wine every weekday. And why would anybody want to watch a stranger bounce their testicles up and down on their wife's face if they weren't at least mildly intoxicated? Liquor was an equaliser, a relaxant, a gateway to recklessness. Without liquor we would be sober and uptight. We would be curious bystanders.

Dress code: smart evening wear ONLY, with 'scanties' and lingerie for the ladies and briefs/boxers for the gentlemen later in the evening.

We knew Alan and Cara's idea of 'smart evening wear' differed wildly to ours. We had seen their photographs online. They tended to favour satin corsets and leather thongs. My boyfriend's idea of smart evening wear involved suit pants and his only pair of Converse without holes.

And finally: NO MEANS NO!

It's not as though I was afraid of being naked in public.

When I started working for a certain youth radio network I felt it only right and fair that I preface my potential employment with a warning regarding my shady past. '*You should probably know*,' I told my future employer with downcast eyes and what I hoped was a genuinely humble expression, '*there are naked photographs of me all over the internet.*' I told them in part probably because I wanted them to think they were getting a real livewire, a tearaway handful at least seven times more fun and interesting than Jane Gazzo; someone who would provide value for money and always keep them on their toes (within legal boundaries). Also I supposed that I feared the moment partway through the year when I felt a tentative tap on the shoulder and heard the words 'Listen, we just got a phone call from Sydney Confidential . . .'

We must all learn a lesson from all those poor idiotic *Big Brother* contestants who walk into a camera-laden compound with a secret and exit two months later to find that a blurry photograph of them topless astride a Weber barbecue has been taken from a *Picture* magazine back issue and plastered all over the newspapers. There were to be no surprises for my employers, no threatening missives made out of cut-out letters arriving in the post and promising to 'reveal all' unless certain demands were met. I would tackle this head on, with aplomb, and with the unspoken and vainglorious suggestion that by posing for naked photos I was somehow that little bit more interesting than anybody else ever.

'She's been a *naked model*?' I imagined my bosses exclaiming to themselves in scandalised tones once I'd swanned from the office in a cloud of deluded bohemian self-worth. 'Aren't we desperately lucky to have acquired her wide-ranging and provocative talents? Aren't we getting ourselves the real deal? I can't wait to hear what she has to say about the new Dizzee Rascal single between 6 and 9 am weekdays!'

I left the pictures online for a long time because I couldn't really care less who saw me naked. The most humiliating photograph was one that showed me rolling around in my underpants pretending to read *The Australian*. The too-tight knickers didn't cause me major concern, but there's no way I wanted to be seen in public reading anything that Greg Sheridan is paid to write op-ed pieces for.

My parents were often naked, and in conversations with friends even now I'm surprised to hear tales of their folks scurrying self-consciously from room to room covering their flesh with oversized beach towels or stretchy t-shirts. Our household was a naked one and I had grown up with a fairly broadminded view on the human body. I found sexuality curious rather than titillating—what people chose to do and why in the privacy of their own homes was of great interest.

Bored one night, my boyfriend had filmed me giving him a blowjob. We watched the footage back together, silently. It wasn't an erotic experience by any stretch of the imagination. I had never seen myself at that angle before, not least partaking in that particular activity. It was like getting the chance to see yourself onstage. After the video finished, my boyfriend turned to me.

'Well? What did you think?'

I studied my face on the screen.

'I never realised,' I said after a thoughtful moment, 'how much I look like my dad.'

Alan and Cara's party was in Kew, near my old high school. I looked out the window of the taxi and watched the hall, where I'd danced onstage with Christie McKay to Bill Medley and Jennifer Warnes's 'The Time of My Life' for the subdued enjoyment of the entire junior school, pass by. I wondered how many people from that assembly hall had taken the path that I was taking now. Perhaps some of them would be in attendance tonight, creating a situation that would rate on the awkward scale somewhere between 'excuse me, I do believe you've taken my umbrella by accident' and 'darling, that was Mr Grainger from number seven. He said you sleepwalked again last night and shat in their hall cupboard.'

We reassured ourselves, in the cab, we weren't committed to *doing* anything. That we could remain curious bystanders at all times.

'If you're in any way uncomfortable,' my boyfriend said, holding my hand, 'we just leave. No questions asked.'

'We're not committed to anything,' I repeated.

'Not a thing,' he replied. 'No contracts, no signatures. Alan and Cara don't know where we live. Let's just go in, have a look around, and see how we feel.'

The house was a tidy, warmly lit terrace. Unobtrusive. We asked the taxi to drop us a little way up the street, as advised.

Please be discreet when entering, the list of rules had reminded us, *and think of our neighbours*.

My friends Sugar and Hotman lived in Collingwood and were convinced their neighbours were swingers.

'What makes you so certain?' I asked them.

'Visitors coming and going at weird hours,' Hotman replied.

'And lots of *couples*,' Sugar added. 'And there are all these . . . weird, awkward hellos at the front door. Like they don't *know* each other well. Except from, you know. Kinky web chats.'

This was a lot of assumption based upon what could simply be a Tupperware party or prayer group and I was too kind to ask Sugar and Hotman what the fuck they were doing watching the door of their neighbours' house with such unnerving intensity anyway. The fact is that we always suspect *something* weird is going on with our neighbours. We hear them fight or have sex and then lie awake under the doona giggling to ourselves about their messy, chaotic lives and how lucky we are not to live there or be in that relationship.

I was once in my study at night having a long and involved phone conversation with Gabi and just as we'd moved onto the topic of what we might be eating for breakfast the next morning there was a startling *bang* of someone's fist on the window facing the street. Fearing a gang of rapists, street urchins or John Hopoate admirers I raced to the back of the house in a mild state of panic.

Tim, I hissed. *I think we're being burgled*.

I had seen the bang as a sort of kindly yet ominous warning; that our home invaders were giving us a chance to neaten ourselves up before they kicked in the front door and beat us to death.

Tim hauled himself reluctantly into action, familiar as he was with late-night proddings along the line of, 'Tim—I think I might have diabetes', and, 'Tim—I think the music of

Fleetwood Mac may no longer be relevant and that fills me with a quiet yet searing sense of despair.'

'Nothing,' he said with a long-suffering sigh when he returned. 'There was *nobody* there. Can I go back to bed now please?'

He later told me he'd received a visit the next day from our neighbour, Brent, who had come over with a sheepish expression.

'My wife told me to apologise . . . I didn't mean to scare your girlfriend,' he mumbled.

Tim was confused. Brent continued.

'It's just that I'm giving up smoking, so my temper's a little . . . you know. And our bedroom is joined to your house. And I know it wasn't that late at night but I was just trying to sleep and she was talking for a long time and I . . . well, when she started talking about rye toast I guess I lost control. I punched the wall. And I'm sorry.'

This should have been comforting—the gangs of rapists and street urchins disappeared in a little overdramatised and slightly embarrassing puff—but all I could think about were the other loud and obnoxious conversations I'd had in my study, unaware that there'd been an audience all along. I'd cried in there—blubberingly, gracelessly, in that way you do when nobody's around to monitor your dignity or admire how pretty you are with one solitary crystalline tear sliding down your porcelain cheek. I'd watched pornography on the laptop not bothering to turn the sound down because Tim wasn't at home. I had confessed secrets and given medical details to doctors. And Brent had been *listening all along*. How mortifying. To this day I don't know who was the worse neighbour.

Alan and Cara's front door was opened by a stony gentleman wearing a dark grey suit. This was clearly 'security'. We presumed that he was paid extra to turn a blind eye. There was likely a whole niche market for sex party security. For the right price they wear an apron and wash up afterwards.

We had done our best not to get there too early ('There's no way I'm standing around for four hours making small talk with Cara about her hall throw,' I had insisted beforehand) and already mingling in Alan and Cara's tastefully decorated living room were about five well-dressed couples, holding glasses of champagne and speaking in polite, muted tones. Alan greeted us like long-lost friends. We'd clearly passed the test.

'Don't you both look *lovely*,' he said, beaming.

Alan himself looked very interesting. He was wearing a pair of leather pants that clung like terrified orphans to his muscular thighs, and a revealing black mesh t-shirt. The outfit seemed at odds with the cream-coloured settee and floral-print curtains.

'Champagne?'

He was carrying a tray laden with flutes. In his leather and mesh outfit he looked like a waiter on a BDSM cruise ship.

'Thanks, Alan, that'd be very nice.'

I didn't know about my boyfriend but my plan was to get as drunk as possible before anything weird happened so I'd be in a better headspace to deal with the absurdity of it. We accepted a glass of champagne and looked around the room with courteous smiles.

'What a nice lounge suite,' my boyfriend said, wisely ignoring the fact that at that moment, directly next to said lounge suite, Alan and Cara's widescreen television was showcasing a video of a not unhappy lady being stuffed full of penis by some willing pool chums.

Outside of the pornography on the television—which, like a racist uncle, the guests seem to be doing their best to ignore—the place was intensely normal. It wasn't gaudy and it wasn't bland. There was no plastic sheeting on the floor. Just a few expensive looking lamps and a mahogany dining table covered with platters of dips and crudités.

'Is that . . . a *cold meat platter*?' I whispered to my boyfriend.

Alan had heard my question.

'Cara loves to feed her guests,' he explained.

I'd never given much thought to the sort of food one would serve at a swingers party. I hadn't really thought about anything but The Moment. That tiny click of transition after everyone had arrived that signalled it was time for the small talk to be over and for the descent into lustful depravity to begin. I was obsessed with The Moment. How did everybody *know* when to start? Was there a bell? Did one particularly forthright partygoer stand up, clap his hands together manfully and say, 'Well, I suppose *I'd* best get stuck in' before coyly revealing his erection?

In pornographic videos, I had seen The Moment occur seamlessly when some doe-eyed blonde giggled naughtily and unzipped a fly, saying 'Why don't we get *these* off.' None of the people around us looked as though they were close to unzipping a fly, their own or anyone else's. They stood around, chatting amiably, like colleagues enjoying a welcome break at a Gold Coast sales conference. It was as though they had no idea they were at a swingers party. They just seemed happy to be at a social gathering with new friends. For a brief moment I wondered if perhaps Alan and Cara had tricked them into coming and we were all about to be a part of some horrifying sex slave ordeal, but the pornography and Alan's revealing outfit seemed to put that theory to bed.

'I won't be playing tonight,' Alan told us with an expression not far from disappointment. 'These nights are more . . . *Cara's* thing. I'm just the host with the most!'

He looked across the room to where Cara stood, laughing outrageously at some quip a strapping young man in a pinstripe shirt had just made. She was wearing a leopard print negligee, a feathered bed jacket and high heels.

'Yeeeep . . . Cara sure loves to play,' he said flatly, not taking his eyes off his lively wife.

Eventually he took us for a tour around the customised downstairs 'area', a lavishly converted basement that would have been the envy of Josef Fritzl.

'So here's our famous circular bed . . . the stripper pole was my wife's idea. She's a playful little thing, like I say! Just you wait and see! Ahahahahaha!'

His leather trousers rubbed together and made a noise like a poorly lubricated goose honking for urgent medical attention.

Lord knows how long it had taken him and Cara to put their sex basement together. One got the sense that Alan had put in all the hard yards while Cara stood in her leopard print negligee, barking instructions. It was a windowless room, decked out with wooden Chinese screens and silk wall hangings. On one side an enormous modified bed—'king-sized' doesn't really do it justice, this thing was essentially two king-sized beds put together—took pride of place, with a chaise longue at its end. ('For the observers,' Alan winked.) The stripper's pole was surrounded by comfortable couches. At the back of the room, the famed 'circular bed'—white leather—sat in dim, foreboding light.

The rest of the room was filled with cushions, mattresses, and two slightly rigid looking massage tables. There was a doorway off to a side room which Alan told us was the 'smoking room—we don't allow cigarettes in the house'. It was so dark we kept bumping into each other, which may have been the intention. You had to admire the effort, though. The place looked terrific. We weren't at some run-of-the-mill, let's-put-the-wipe-and-wear-Twister-mat-down-and-take-it-from-there sex night for amateurs. These people had done this before. A lot. When it came to swingers parties, they were the Calvin Kleins of the scene.

Upstairs, the conversation twirled in light, balletic circles. Obviously people wanted to know each other well before the night unfolded, but not *too* well.

'So you work in . . . ?'

'Media.'

'Right.'

It was as though we were spies, trained in the art of speaking around a conversation. Or enjoying a game of Hangman ('Is there a letter . . . A?'). I didn't want somebody I was having a conversation with to suddenly widen their eyes and say, 'You mean Marieke Hardy from *The Age*?' So I sidestepped. And so did they. A handsome older man wearing expensive jewellery told me he ran a live music venue in St Kilda.

'Oh, I see a lot of live music,' I said enthusiastically. 'Which venue is it?'

He looked instantly cagey.

'Just a venue,' he replied. 'You probably wouldn't know it.'

Eventually the conversation about what a nice apartment we were in ran dry and we both looked away awkwardly, which was no small feat considering the most prominent thing in our eyeline was *Anal Invaders 8* on the wide-screen television.

I pointed, figuring I may as well acknowledge what was going on directly in front of our faces.

'She certainly seems to be enjoying herself,' I said clumsily. He looked at me and edged away. Perhaps I had committed a faux pas. Nobody was allowed to talk about sex until the sex was actually occurring. This was a fairly impossible task.

It came as a relief to know my boyfriend and I weren't the only ones new to the experience. There were about eight other amateurs, all looking as nervous and inept as us. One younger couple picked us as newbies—possibly due to the fact I had started giggling hysterically—and sidled up, sensing with relief that we would be from that moment on friends and confidantes.

'All *I* want to know,' whispered the girl to me, 'is when it *starts*.'

She was wearing a tight satin evening dress and heavy eye makeup. I took her to be about twenty-four years old. Her boyfriend was shorter than her, one of those boys in their mid-twenties who look about twelve. He had acne and was wearing a dreadful comedy tie. His leg jiggled nervously.

'I mean, is there a bell or something?' he said impatiently.

Around the room, all the other newcomers shifted shyly with sidelong glances. They had come here for a deeply pornographic experience, not a garden tea. And yet here we were, chatting gaily about our day jobs, or aspects of them ('I'm not going to tell you exactly what I do, but you can guess. Here's a clue. It rhymes with Pairplane Filot'), and passing around trays of finger sandwiches. It was like being at dancing classes in year seven when all you could do was gaze agonisingly across the room at all the members of the sex you weren't allowed to touch. One young man was offered a breadstick by Alan and actually blushed.

Swingers parties have a fairly low rate of returning guests, which is both a comforting and alarming fact. Obviously the majority of couples only dip their toe in the depraved world of partner swapping once and return to their ordinary lives, curiosity sated. They carry on their existence, allowing the memory of group sex to fade to a comfortable anecdote. This was clearly preferable to those who made a career of it, selling precious family heirlooms in order to fund their latest kinky episode. The last thing anybody wants to see at a swingers party is a pair of sixty-year-olds wearing vinyl teddies and saying, 'Don't worry, you're in safe hands' with leering, suggestive smiles.

Then again, I wondered why there *were* suspiciously so many fresh faces at Alan and Cara's soiree. What occurred in that downstairs garage to ensure that over half of last month's guests hadn't come back? Were we to skin a goat alive and stand in a circle singing Skyhooks songs while Alan sodomised its corpse? 'I'm just the host with the most!' The question '*what exactly constitutes "too far" at a swingers party?*' kept rattling through my brain. I wished I'd kept a copy of the rules handy.

But when did it start, when did it start? I saw my boyfriend look at his watch. He glanced up at me and shrugged. It was now nine-thirty. We had been there for over an hour, eating olives and talking to people about what they didn't do for a living. This tortured exercise in June Dally-Watkins etiquette could only go on for so long.

A couple in the smoking room had quite clearly flaunted

the no drugs policy and were speaking to everybody who entered at high speed and volume, flitting from topic to topic like a pair of amphetamine-addled hummingbirds. One of them had a bloody nose, which he cheerfully wiped away without a second thought. I wondered if the security guard would step in at any point and request they move into the time out corner until they'd both had the chance to calm down. I didn't blame them for wanting to alter reality. At that point I was so on edge I was tempted to ask them where they'd purchased their powders and if they'd mind ever so much sharing their stash around.

We were lingering in the hallway, discussing in muted tones whether we should leave, when a small group burst through the front door. An Amazonian woman dressed in a trench coat led the way, followed by a smaller woman with cropped hair and spectacles, who looked oddly like the cartoon character Penfold from 1980s children's TV series *Danger Mouse*. Behind them stood a rake-thin ghoulish man with a pencil moustache. They were a no-nonsense blast of energy, nodding a curt hello to Alan and without any further ado making their way downstairs. Everyone watched them go, stunned.

'Ah,' said Alan, pleased. 'Anita's here.'

And then one of the young men we had spoken to previously crept up from downstairs. His excitement was palpable. He looked like Ginger Meggs having just been told he was about to have a one-on-one training session with Don Bradman.

'It's started!' he squealed in a high-pitched, thrilled voice.

Meggs was right: it *had* started. We edged our way down into the garage to find that the charming 'Well, *I* find Earth First is best when really trying to get rid of stubborn stains' middle-class dinner party from upstairs had turned into Sodom and Gomorrah. In the semi-darkness, we could see five bodies writhing on the satin bed. The amphetamine-fuelled couple from the smoking room did everything but shout 'STACKS ON', and flung themselves into the mix with abandon. A girl who looked like Lily Allen twirled shyly and slowly around the stripper's pole while her proud boyfriend looked on. In the corner, just out of view, somebody was already making a spectacular amount of noise on the round bed. We edged our way towards it, stepping over the anarchy of flesh.

'I do believe,' I said in hushed, reverent tones to my boyfriend when our eyes adjusted, 'that nice lady in the trench coat over there is being fisted.'

There she was, spreadeagled on the bed, while her bespectacled companion held a sideways human rights rally up her vagina. She was emitting a series of wails and moans but nobody much looked as though they were enjoying themselves. They all wore expressions of intense concentration, as though studying for an upcoming fisting exam at the Vagina Academy. We stood to one side, staring in amazement, curious bystanders waiting for a bus that would never come.

Everywhere around us people were starting to strip off with eager little panting noises. A man brushed past me and I felt his naked genitals sweep against my dress with a soft little swish. It was kill or be killed at this point. My boyfriend had a panicked 'I need an adult' look on his face. Everything about what was happening seemed so forced; twenty or so very ordinary people in a suburban garage suddenly acting on cue as though they were Traci Lords. Surely they couldn't have all been feeling so sexy so fast. We'd only just finished our Jatz crackers. I felt the panic as the social niceties I adhered to slipped away. There was no point of reference for this.

My boyfriend whispered to me. He looked unhappy.

'Should we . . . ?'

'Should we what? Leave? Join in the five-way currently taking place on the massage table?'

He shrugged, not enjoying the moment any more than I.

'Should we do *something*?' he breathed eventually.

We moved into a corner and started kissing, not really certain what else was expected of us. I squeezed my eyes shut and tried to pretend that directly behind me a Roman orgy wasn't taking place, which was difficult considering someone with a very high-pitched voice kept saying, 'That's the stuff, that's the stuff' over and over again. I wondered, briefly, if Ginger Meggs had scored.

A man appeared behind us. He tapped my boyfriend on the shoulder.

'Do you mind if I . . . ?'

It was as though he were cutting in on us at Lord and Lady Swarthington's summer ball. I had half a mind to fan myself coquettishly and drop a hanky on the floor, though this would have been intensely difficult since I was dressed by this stage only in my underpants.

I looked at my boyfriend. This was it, the chance to really take the step and be active participants in a swingers party. No longer curious bystanders. We didn't know this man. We would never meet him again. And he was standing there expectantly, with an erection you could comfortably dangle a small child off. He was smiling pleasantly.

'Take your time,' he said, or his penis seemed to. 'We're all adults here.'

As we left, we passed Alan. He was washing glasses in the kitchen and humming a little tune to himself. He turned when he heard us come up the stairs and looked pleased for the company.

'Ah!' he said brightly. 'Can I top up your glasses?'

'Actually, Alan . . . we were just leaving.'

He looked disappointed.

'Already?'

'It's not that it wasn't a wonderful party. We're just . . . tired.'

Alan nodded in resignation. Perhaps he sensed that we might never come back, that we may join the ranks of those other fly-by-nighters, briefly adventurous pioneers more comfortable in the realm of the ordinary. He and Cara would play host to a revolving door of new faces, ever younger and more nervous than the last.

He expressed curiosity as to what point proceedings had reached downstairs—I believe his words were 'what's shakin' in the basement'—and when we told him about the woman being fisted his face fell.

'Oh *no*,' he wailed. 'I have *told* her a *thousand* times . . .'

We must have looked startled. He dried his hands on his apron and started rummaging beneath the sink as he explained his distress.

'She's a *squirter*,' he said. 'I mean, I'm all for people coming around and having their fun. That's what we're here for. But I say to her, "Anita, somebody has to clean that up, you know." And it's always me, isn't it? It's always old Alan, having to clean up the mess.'

He seemed flustered and upset, pulling out from beneath the sink a couple of sponges and a bucket. We bid him farewell and he waved distractedly, his mind on other things. As we left we could hear the sound of music downstairs. The odd bellow rang out, but there were no sounds of joy. Nobody was laughing.

The cab rounded the corner. I rested my head on my boyfriend's shoulder and we talked sleepily about the night's proceedings. Next month Alan and Cara would play host to a new batch of strangers and we would be returned to our pedestrian existence, smiling politely at the peccadilloes of the swing set. We knew we would never return.

Behind us my old high school sat placid in the darkness. I didn't look back.

YTT

I get the private message on Facebook, of course, of course. The technological town crier of my generation heralds news of births and mourns deaths and rings the bells of change to the point where a day without some kind of electronic revelation seems almost disappointing.

'I'm hoping you may be able to solve one of the greatest mysteries of my lifetime so far.'

This is an intriguing beginning to a message. No less significant is the fact it seems free from subsequent pleas for the transferring of money to Nigerian 'benk' accounts or the bone-chilling sentence 'So that's about when I realised we had the same father.'

The message is from a friend I was glued to long ago. The word 'glued' undervalues the semi-psychotic devotion of our friendship. Susan and I practically lived inside each other. We spent every day together from 1986 to 1988 with a love nothing less than religious. The friendships of prepubescence invite no lighthearted commitment. You embody each other's skin. Physically you may look nothing alike but elderly relatives insist they can't tell you apart, and you enter rooms clutching each other around the waist or neck with a fierce sense of ownership.

'I'm hoping you may be able to solve one of the greatest mysteries of my lifetime so far.'

Immediately I know I've done something wrong, been involved somehow. Was I part of some rape cover-up, standing around like a beer-swilling accomplice in *The Accused*? 'One of the greatest mysteries of my lifetime so far' sounds deeply important.

People like to make jokes about their forgetfulness. 'I'm so darned . . . absent-minded!' they exclaim with adorable shrugs, which can make memory loss sound very sweet and endearing though in my experience there's very little endearing about standing bewilderedly in the middle of a living-room shouting 'WHAT THE FUCK AM I SUPPOSED TO BE DOING IN HERE??' particularly if it's the living room of a complete stranger and you have wandered in wild-eyed off the street like Robert Downey Jr.

Yes, everybody sometimes forgets their keys, or the name of their boss's wife ('Oh god, I think I called her Sandra. Wasn't Sandra the name of his *second* wife? I am totally getting fired on Monday'), or the easy-to-neglect fact that if you leave hot oil on the stove you will very probably burn your house down. A small amount of memory loss is normal. Spend an hour trying to remember where your car is parked at Chadstone Shopping Centre, fine. Sit up with a horrified gasp at 3 am realising that not only have you forgotten your mother's birthday but *you were supposed to bake the cake*, understandable. A small amount of memory loss is daffy and darling and a defining character trait for girls who stick pencils in their hair or use phrases like 'aw, baloney'.

My memory loss ranges somewhere between 'oh dear, I seem to have left the house without any pants on again' and Mickey Rooney, a man who, if his fake Twitter account is to be believed, spends his downtime asking questions like 'Why am I eating this cake? Why am I wearing a party hat? Why are people singing at me?' and 'What's a volcano? Can I have two soft tacos? What's a taco?' Why anyone would look to me for answers requiring a delve down memory lane is beyond comprehension. And yet here she was, after twenty years, my Susan.

In 1987 Susan was a lanky streak of bacon, with a neat bob she did up in a spiky, Pat Benatar-inspired ponytail, and awesome big round spectacles like that secretary character Janine used to wear in *Ghostbusters*. She was Greek, which meant when I was eleven I wanted to be Greek too. I craved the exotic oiliness of the culture, the salt and the religious icons and the shouty father figures who emitted comforting aromas of tobacco and ouzo. I even insisted my parents let me temporarily attend Susan's weekend Greek school, where I spent a few entirely happy afternoons sitting in a corner smiling like an idiot and not knowing what the fuck anybody else was talking about. They eventually banned me from attending after I came home using the word *malaka* in its correct context but I was still allowed to spend many contented afternoons at Susan's house listening to her parents arguing in their dense, prickly language. I fell in love with Susan because she was bright and funny and she didn't find it weird that I thought Harriet the Spy was a real person.

Together we posed awkwardly for home-made *Dolly* magazine modelling shots and told ourselves we were definitely prettier than Kate Fischer or Anneliese Seubert, not realising that we weren't and never would be and it didn't matter. We re-enacted the moody, soft-focus photographs we'd pored over around her parents' swimming pool, wearing elastic headbands and Esprit leather jackets and high-waisted snow-wash denim.

'You could be the next Alison Brahe . . . but, you know, a Greek version,' I told Susan, privately hoping that this clearly overblown compliment would lead to equally lavish praise for me.

It was around this time we discovered a television program called *Young Talent Time*, a music-driven Channel Ten series that would these days probably be pulled unceremoniously from air for promoting child rape or slave labour or something equally sinister. Each episode consisted of eight or nine milk-fed little poplettes dressed in lycra halternecks and ra-ra skirts butchering chart hits of the day ('Celebrate' by Kool & the Gang was a well-abused favourite) before gathering around ageing '70s disc jockey John 'call me Johnny, it's not creepy in any way whatsoever' Young and singing the Beatles song 'All My Loving' in what I suppose in some lesser-evolved countries would consider unison. The night ended when a random petrified child chosen from the audience looked down the barrel of a camera and shrieked 'GOODNIGHT AUSTRALIA' and the producers cut to a plastic model of a McDonald's restaurant with a toy car parked out the front.

I recently sat through an entire episode on YouTube and was appalled by how truly awful it all was. There was even someone on the show named 'Bevan'. Yet in 1987 Susan and I saw none of *YTT*'s garish, plasticky hideousness, its shrill posturing or borderline uncomfortable song choices ('When I Kissed The Teacher'?, 'Get Outta My Dreams, Get Into My Car'?). We were completely bewitched. Every Saturday night at 6 pm we would go into lockdown, sitting breathless and cross-legged in front of the television. Dutifully we would videotape each episode and then dissect it at length during the week ('Why do you think Johnny introduced Juanita's song but not Greg's? Do you think maybe Greg is going to get sacked because he's an albino with buck teeth?') before applying ourselves to learning the dance routines by heart and performing them in the backyard with barefoot gusto, undeterred by the threat of bindies.

This, in itself, is not an unusual experience for a young lady of my years. It's fairly common these days to be at a party with peers and mention the words *Young Talent Time* only to find yourself three hours later in a heated group debate about whether Vince Del Tito was fucking Dannii 'two I's are better to see you with!' Minogue or Natalie Miller. *YTT* was a

Saturday night ritual for most Australian children and in that, I suppose, Susan and I were no different from anybody else. We did, however, take things a step further by starting an official fan club for one of the members.

Let's call him Joey Dee. Because that's his name. Or maybe it isn't, I don't know, there was a confusing period where we were convinced he'd shortened it from something elaborately Italian 'for showbiz reasons'. We spent hours and hours—and possibly hundreds of dollars—crammed into the phone booth on Tooronga Road going through all the possibilities in the *White Pages* and calling them up.

'Hello, is that . . . Mrs Dimattina?' I would say in a trembling voice. 'Would . . . Joey possibly be at home?'

To all the nice families with Italian surnames who received irritating phone calls from two giggling twits in the late 1980s: I apologise. Lord knows what we would have done if by some miracle of nature we'd chanced upon the real Joey Dee's number and he'd come to the phone to say hello. Most likely we would have shrieked like Toni Childs gargling acid and hung up, which is how most phone calls to boys ended in 1987. If we had used our collective organisational powers for good instead of idiocy we could have probably done something worthwhile with our lives. As it was we mooned over this bright, gap-toothed, fairly average twelve-year-old boy with a mullet hairdo as though he was Christ himself.

Joey Dee wasn't what you'd call particularly memorable. Out of all the boys on the show—Vince, Bevan, Greg, Jamie, Johnny and the criminally dull Tim—I can recall no real reason we picked him as our own personal Jesus. He sang semi-decently and was proficient in a few basic Michael Jackson moves, a skill no doubt he'd picked up early on in life to counterbalance any schoolyard accusations of faggotry. He had a very sweet little diastema and a diligently maintained feathery mullet and lovely green eyes. He was average in every sense.

The amount of projected fantasy character traits adolescent girls are able to slather upon innocent young boys is truly frightening. At twelve years of age, most boys are into burping, punching each other in the face, and delightedly finding new and inventive ways to touch their penises without anybody else noticing. More luck to them, I say. Yet in the minds of certain young ladies—particularly those who have spent perhaps a smidgen too long memorising weighty intellectual tomes such as *Sweet Valley High*—these boys are nothing short of poets. If they appear to stumble over their words, it is not because they are drooling lunkheads attempting to peer down our t-shirts. It is simply because they're struggling to find the right sonnet with which to win our hearts. If they hock a sodden spitball directly into our faces when we mount the school bus of a morn, it's not because they think such an act is *amusing*. They are simply shy bohemians, sad clowns letting their clumsy overtures of courtship speak the words they cannot say.

Joey Dee never stood a chance. Simply through absorbing his chirpy exchanges with Johnny Young, his sparkly, high-energy performances, and every minute detail of his time on screen, we had pieced together a personality so far from reality it was almost obscene. Without ever speaking a word to him we had created a fictionalised robo-boy who catered emotionally to our every sweeping need. In our minds, Joey Dee was a quiet, polite young man with a penchant for soft-serve ice creams and holding hands. He disdained buffoonery and horseplay and could think of no greater way to spend an afternoon than curled up on the couch watching *Labyrinth*. After which he would learn all the song and dance routines with us and fall about laughing as we tried together to practice 'Dance Magic Dance' in front of the bedroom mirror. He would appear shyly on our porch, holding a dewy rose and murmuring the only sort of poetry we'd had access to thus far. Stock, Aitken and Waterman lyrics played a huge part in this. With big doe eyes fixed upon ours, he'd sigh the lyrics to 'I Should Be So Lucky' and 'Love in the First Degree'.

During sleepovers, late at night, we would lie awake and take turns making up stories about Joey Dee falling desperately in love with us and wanting to kiss us on our faces. We were at that beautifully innocent sexual precipice where we knew we *wanted* boys but we had no idea what to do with them once we got them. There was a vague idea of gentle hand-holding and butterflies in the stomach, but the thought of anything more erotic just produced confusing feelings like when we watched that Darth Vader 'let's do it on the moon' scene in *Revenge of the Nerds* and went very quiet.

Our sleepover stories would describe elaborate scenarios, story arcs and occasional meddling from jealous female members of the Team, but they always ended the same: with one of us wrapped firmly in Joey's muscular arms, safe from the trials and tribulations of the world.

'Joey saw you across the crowd at Luna Park,' I would begin, whispering into the night, 'and he knew he had to get with you.'

I guess you could call it erotic fan fiction. But we were too young to understand exactly what that was. You should have seen us there, side-by-side in the darkness, clenched tight in separate sleeping bags. Our stories grew more and more fantastical—there were platinum records, weddings, immaculately conceived babies. The fan club was a natural extension of this, though we had of course no idea how to run such an organisation. As an only child I was adept at bossing people around and took it upon myself to bully schoolmates into paying the dollar joining fee.

'What's a Joey Dee?' they would say. 'Why am I giving you a dollar? If I give it to you do you promise to go away and leave me alone?'

Susan and I rabidly collected names and money. We took no prisoners. Four-year-old cousins became members of The Official Joey Dee Fan Club. So did parents, uncles and long-suffering older siblings. Mrs Moy, the lollipop lady at our school who was part deaf and occasionally wet her pants whilst helping people cross the road, became a member. Certainly she may have been under the impression she was donating to the Red Cross, but that's neither here nor there. We took her urine-scented dollar coin and we added it to the tissue box that served as our coffers. Joey Dee deserved commitment and two dedicated fan club co-presidents willing to lay down and die for him. We were made for this.

His mother loved us. Why wouldn't she? We validated her adoration for her son, turning up at Channel Ten Nunawading wearing homemade WE ♥ JOEY badges and falling apart in fits of frothing hysterics from within the depths of a startled family audience. Eventually we conned our way backstage and stood, breathless and flattened against the wall in case somebody noticed and threw us out. We watched with wide eyes as clothes racks of costumes trundled past, nudged each other when one of the dance instructors gave us a wink, and shared conspiratorial sick faces the moment the much-loathed Tim approached with a friendly grin and asked if we wanted him to sign anything.

Courtney Compagnino was cuter than us, more talented than us, and a star of the show, so we made it a point to hate her guts too. 'She's so *fat*,' we would say snidely from the comfort of our living-room chairs as Courtney's bright little face hit the screens. 'She's a *fat slut*.' We would cut the eyes out of her photographs and draw cartoonish oversized boobs in texta on her face in a technique that would these days likely be considered a criminal offence if employed by an older gentleman with perhaps too much time on his hands. This was a ten-year-old child we were tearing apart, although at eleven we could hardly be expected to behave as moral compasses. Courtney Compagnino was a girl who had unrestricted access to Joey Dee and was therefore the enemy.

In our colourfully inventive sleepover stories she had so far been variously set alight, run over by a truck, and torn apart by wolves. Yet when we were introduced to her by a kindly stagehand, we were nothing short of fawning.

'Oh, I love your *hair*,' we cooed. 'Do you use your own crimper or do they do it in makeup before the show?'

Inch by inch, Saturday by Saturday, we moved closer to Joey Dee. Like the worst kind of suck-ups we giggled at the Assistant Director's bad jokes, made cups of tea for the choreographers, and tolerated tedious drawn-out conversations with Tim. ('So what did you guys think of my routines tonight? Did you have a fave?') Throughout it all we'd catch glimpses of Joey, gliding from dressing room to green room, sharing private conversations with a friendly crew member, surreptitiously touching up his hair in a corridor mirror. Susan was the first to target Joey's smiling, broad-faced mama, making a beeline and explaining in her gentle, polite way that we were his number one fans and would love to say hello.

Joey's mother eyed us with nothing short of unbridled delight.

'Fan club?' she exclaimed. 'You two *must* come over to our place for a visit!'

Well, I don't recall if there was a tussle back at Susan's house. I don't recall if a date was made and she was busy or her strict father wouldn't let her skip Greek school or if I simply just manipulated the whole thing so she couldn't make it and I went alone because I am a selfish cur. It's likely.

There were tears. Mine were probably of the guilty

variety. I felt bad for muscling Susan out of the arrangement, but it was obvious to me that *I needed to be alone with Joey Dee*. Susan and I were best friends, yes, but even best friends can be cumbersome when true love is on the cards. She knew me too well, could see clearly when I was embellishing stories to make myself look more impressive. She'd be able to cut me down halfway through an anecdote by cheerily reminding me that's not how it happened *at all* and even utter the mortifying phrase all too common to my ears: 'Marieke, you're just showing off.' The truth was, as a control freak I felt I knew how to do everything better than anyone else, and that included winning Joey Dee's heart. I loved Susan to bits but I couldn't bring myself to relinquish power. I told myself I would make up for it by inviting her to our wedding. She could be my main bridesmaid. We would name our child after her, even if it were a boy. On it went, this plodding, twisted internal monologue attempting to justify the fact that I'd essentially just shunted my favourite girlfriend out of the way so I could get my sticky paws on a pre-teen fantasy we'd created and craved for together.

Susan, none the wiser—or maybe she was and just forgave me for it, which is even worse—made me promise to tell her *every tiny detail*, from the moment the front door opened and I was welcomed inside the hallowed portal of the Dee household, to the part where Joey and I hugged goodbye on the lawn and promised to be friends forever so long as I introduced him to my amazing friend Susan who sounded like great fun.

'*Everything*,' she implored with agonised wails. 'Take *notes*.'

The Dee family lived in Altona South, a suburb that in 1987 was a curious mixture of migrant McMansions, Vietnamese fruit markets and illegal street racing. Their house was big and broad and brown, a sprawling teacake with a beautifully manicured strip of lawn barricading the front. Joey's mother answered the door and wiped her hands on a worn apron.

'Here she is! Where's your little friend with the glasses?'

My heart was beating so loud it was in my ears. I could feel it throbbing through my lobes. It was like *Innerspace* meets *Tap Dogs*.

'She . . . couldn't make it.' Hardy, you worm. You liar. You snake.

'That's a pity. Come in, darling.'

Darling. I was family already.

She led me in, past the obligatory gilt-edged entrance hall. The house was warm and buttery. I exhaled deeply. I had transferred my love of the exotic European abode neatly from Susan's compact Hawthorn digs to Joey's spacious Altona South residence. I pictured myself spending happy afternoons here eating liquor-soaked cake and swinging my legs at the dining table and sucking up to Joey's parents in a toadying way. Joey's father sat in a La-Z-Boy recliner wearing socks and velour slippers. He grunted at me upon introduction. I was bustled into the kitchen and offered a variety of comestibles, all of which I politely declined. I wanted to stay minty fresh.

'JOEY! COME DOWNSTAIRS, YOU HAVE A VISITOR!'

Slouching downstairs in stockinged feet—by which of course I mean socks, not that he suddenly appeared in a stay-up fishnet and suspenders combo; it's just that the word 'socked' looks insufferably stupid—and scowling heavily at the interruption to his afternoon's Gameboy activities, he was shorter than I remembered. The lack of layered on pancake makeup made him seem pale and slightly sickly. A bristle of pre-pubescent moustache scattered across his upper lip like hair confetti. He wore Mambo boardshorts and had a carpet burn on one knee. He regarded me curiously, as though I was a long-forgotten thought he'd once entertained and hadn't bothered to recall since.

'Hey,' he mumbled.

I opened my mouth but nothing came out. The sound of the harness racing on the television provided a comforting cushion of background noise. There was a pause as we studied each other.

'Go on then, Joe,' his mother said encouragingly. 'Take Marika up to your room.'

I wasn't going to correct her. People always got my name wrong and if my future mother-in-law wanted to refer to me as 'Marika' then I was happy to change it by deed poll. I would have changed it to 'Fuckface'. I would have tattooed a picture of a donkey on my forehead and joined NAMBLA at that point, I would have done anything. I was here, I was in his house. It was happening. Oh, Joey Dee. Oh, Joe.

Joey nodded the invitation and headed back up the stairs. I performed the obligatory 'it's a lovely house you have here,

Mr Dee, Mrs Dee' before meekly following. The corridor smelt of carpet-cleaning powder and ducted heating. Joey slammed from wall to wall as he walked, in that curious way that young boys have, and kicked open a door with a crude gold star stuck to the front.

I sat on his bed (Where else would I sit? The desk? What was I going to do, take a letter? Oh god, this was too much) and watched politely as he shuffled around his bedroom, pointing out his belongings as though I had arrived from the *Guinness Book of Records* office and demanded to jot down an inventory.

'So . . . this is my guitar. This is my Matchbox car collection. This is my invisible dog leash, I got it at the Royal Melbourne Show. See, it looks like you're walking a dog but there's *no dog*,' he ventured as I nodded and pretended to show an interest.

Wow, I thought. *Famous people can be so down-to-earth.*

Clearly bored by my presence, he hummed tunelessly under his breath, staring for a long time at a gently fluttering mobile of an aeroplane on his ceiling, before turning suddenly to look at me.

'Wanna watch me play drums?'

'Sure,' I said.

'I'm pretty good.'

'I bet.'

True to his word, Joey sat down at his drum kit and performed a seventeen minute drum solo. I studied his face as he played. I had pored over that face from every possible angle.

I had wept over his photographs and crudely paused him, mid-song, so I could mournfully paw at his frozen, distorted features on the television.

'Would you watch the fucking video properly?' my mother would say, irritated by my pathetic mewling. 'You're leaving fingerprints on the screen.'

And here he was, right in front of me, in the flesh. Concentrating as he bashed out some interminable rhythm. He just looked so . . . ordinary.

I should be enjoying this, I thought with a quiet desperation. All these months of planning and pining and practising what I would say when he turned up on my porch with the rose and now I was sitting here with a trickle of Impulse Body Mist making its way from my hairless armpit to my waist and wondering just how long I could tolerate this nightmare before I called my mother and implored her to come and pick me up. I was intimidated. I was weirded out. Worst of all, I was bored.

'Watch this,' Joey commanded, before spinning one drumstick around and around in his fingers.

Eventually after what seemed like hours of aimless banging he tired himself out and lurched from his drum kit. There was a tense silence as he mooched his way around his bedroom, looking for something to do. I sat on my hands and prayed for intervention. How does one make small talk with an idol, particularly one who so rapidly seems to have become a mere mortal? I knew all of his likes (Michael Jackson, playing drums, mum's cooking) and dislikes (homework, mean people). I knew his star sign (Cancer) and his favourite colour (yellow). I was embarrassed about the fan club and confused by how different Joey Dee was in reality to the swoonworthy rose-carrier of our creation. I stood, ready to make polite noises about heading back home.

And that's when he lunged over and kissed me.

We fell back onto his bed, Joey writhing clumsily in what was presumably the throes of childish passion and me frozen in a state of blind panic.

'Kiss me!' he whispered wetly into my forehead.

The only kissing I had done so far was underwater with my neighbour Jono Andrews when we were both five and 'practising breathing'. I had imagined softness and sweetness and the scent of freshly washed laundry. And yet here I was with the boy of my dreams licking at my face like an overexcited Labrador. He meant well—by which I mean he was being in no way rapey—and was giggling in a friendly, high-pitched fashion like Ben Mendelsohn in *The Year My Voice Broke.* I giggled too, hysterically—I was utterly terrified by this point—and playfully attempted to slip from his grasp.

'Hee hee!' I screamed shrilly. 'Let's probably not do that anymore!!!'

Joey got the message and slumped back on to his pillows, instantly bored again. It was obvious he had no idea of what use I may be to him. I was a poor conversationalist, I hadn't appreciated his brilliant musicianship. And I wouldn't even make the afternoon lively by indulging in a little light petting. Why I'd bothered to visit in the first place seemed utterly beyond him.

There was a long and terse silence while I adjusted my Sportsgirl windcheater.

'Well . . . I better do some drum practice.'

I nodded.

'Of course.'

I made my way carefully down to the kitchen again and spent a not entirely comfortable forty minutes eating a tray of biscuits and listening to the distant sounds of Joey taking out his aggression on a presumably terrified snare drum. I was dazed. Mrs Dee seemed apologetic for her son's pressing percussive schedule cutting our visit short.

'Joe's a busy boy,' she said softly.

'That's okay, Mrs Dee! I've had a great time! Really! Thank you so much for having me!' I managed brightly, hoping that my parents would show up before I started crying.

Nobody could get anything out of me about my visit. My parents were surprised by my uncharacteristic silence, and couldn't understand why I wasn't in a hurry to see Susan. She, too, seemed hurt by my standoffishness. When I eventually saw her I played down the visit as 'stupid' and tried to encourage a cooling off from Joey Dee ('I think I like River Phoenix better anyway'), which she found mystifying. It was the first real wedge driven between us, and it indelibly bruised us both.

Despite our best intentions we ended up at different high schools and no matter how much we swore never to let that change things, it did. I fell in with a simpering crowd of private school hair flickers who bullied me mercilessly and Susan seemed to breeze through with new loud-talking Camberwell High classmates and invitations to pool parties. We called each other every night, and then a few times a week, and eventually only every now and then. I became ashamed of our childish love for *Young Talent Time* and wanted it to remain secret. I couldn't admit the Joey Dee obsession to the sophisticated new set I was desperate to be accepted by. In the light of their eyes it seemed freakish. We were too old for such things. Susan became a problematic emblem of a past from which I was trying to wrestle myself free.

On the rare occasions we saw each other I felt like she came from a distant planet I'd long ago visited and I would look at the face that I'd known and loved so well and her new, more adult, glasses and I couldn't think of anything to say.

'I wonder what Joey Dee would be up to these days,' I'd try out in a jokey voice, but it sounded as trite as I suspected it would and we both fell silent.

Strange how I remember all these *Young Talent Time* adventures now. Fragments of them, anyway. The rest I piece together, or make up to suit whatever crowd I'm attempting to impress with tales of my childhood.

'Did I ever tell you,' I start, 'about the time I ran a fan club for *Joey Dee* from *Young Talent Time*?' and everybody obligingly screeches with mocking laughter.

Susan became less and less a part of these retellings, and with passing years I edited her from our story altogether.

Then twenty years on, the Facebook message arrives, and a jolt back to feeling everything anew.

I'm hoping you may be able to solve one of the greatest mysteries of my lifetime so far.

When I finally pluck up the courage to call her she has the sunny, tired, motherly voice of someone always interrupting a conversation with the words 'for god's sake put that *down*' and tells me she's so sorry to bother me.

'I know you're busy,' she says. 'I've read about you in the paper.'

Hardly a comforting beginning. The last time I appeared in the paper I was being slapped across the wrist for daring to suggest that simpering Liberal politician Christopher Pyne was perhaps not the most likeable chap on the face of the earth.

'Still making an unbridled idiot of myself,' I rue aloud and she laughs, and it's suddenly so familiar and two decades disappear in blessed moments. She calls herself 'Sue' these days, something I can't get used to. We talk about Joey Dee ('I hear he's a hairdresser now,' I enjoy telling her, listening to her scandalised gasps) and her parents (both well), her husband and her child.

'This is going to sound stupid . . .' she starts off with an apologetic chuckle, then launches into the real purpose for her making contact.

She wants answers to a long ago conundrum, and she has come to me. This will not go well. The doors of my memory are closing in the most terrifying of ways, slamming shut with clanging finality behind me like the credits of *Get Smart*. There are gaping holes where there should be anecdotes and pain and remorse. The lines between truth and fiction are so smeared I sometimes can't remember if I was actually friends with the Goonies or whether they were just characters in a movie.

I argue with an old male friend about whether we slept together or not when we were teenagers. He insists we didn't. I insist we did. He laughs, appalled.

'You think I wouldn't *remember* if we'd had sex?' he bellows so loudly that a nearby mother places protective palms over her fascinated child's ears.

I run into ex-beaus, offer them friendly, hail-fellow-well-met smiles, and can't understand why they coolly dismiss me and walk away. I must have done something dreadful. Lord knows I'm capable of it. But what? I can't remember. I have blocked it from my mind and replaced it with something pop-culture-ish and fatuous like the name of the lead singer from Soul Asylum (Dave Pirner) or various Beastie Boys lyrics. It's as though there's no room for important memories when there's so much vapid information clamouring to be let in. 'Bad break-ups? Infidelity? Hurtful arguments? We won't be needing *those* anymore,' I imagine my brain deciding with cheery insistence, like an efficient mother preparing for a garage sale. 'Let's just memorise the names of Gwyneth Paltrow's ex-boyfriends in order instead!'

Over coffee one day, Gen mentions a Japanese restaurant in the city we'd visited a while ago. I don't remember it.

'Oh, *you* know,' she says with a bored insistence. 'It's that noisy place in the laneway where we had that fight.'

Fight? Gen is one of my dearest friends. We have minor irritations with each other, emotional scuffles solved hours later with a texting pun-war and wine-soaked embrace at Joe's Shoe Store. We don't *fight*.

'What fight?'

She looks at me as if I am joking. I half smile back at her, suspecting like any decent dementia sufferer that I'm being played for a fool.

'Ha! There *was* no fight,' I say triumphantly. 'You're making it up!'

Gen looks even more aghast now. My smile fades.

'Marieke, there was a *fight*. You got really mad at me and we practically didn't speak for two months.'

I don't think she's joking. But then I can't believe she's serious. I have utterly no recollection of this event and am convinced that I would remember something as important as fighting with a best pal and cutting off communication for eight weeks. Perhaps Gen has gone insane and this is the first warning signal.

'You really don't remember that? It was huge. We never *not speak*.'

'I know!'

There's an explanation required now. Something so drastic should not be forgotten. This is an important mark on our friendship. It is a hurt we should be able to call on lest it ever occur again. That I have obviously pressed on in life without giving it a second thought says a lot about my shallow personality.

'I've probably pushed it from my mind,' I make up on the spot, 'because it takes me to a dark place.'

Gen is unconvinced.

'I just find it strange. That you would forget something like that.'

'Gen,' I try to catch her eye now. My tone drops to a confidential hum. 'I think there's something really wrong. *With my memory.*'

When my spelling starts going too I know I'm in trouble. I find myself staring in bewilderment at my mobile telephone, too stubborn and confused and proud to use predictive text ('I prefer doing *my own* spelling,' I regularly and loftily inform uninterested friends), and wondering exactly when it was I forgot how to spell the word 'grateful'.

It's probably the liquor and the music festivals. I glumly recall the year I staggered around Meredith at nine in the morning offering people free shots of vodka and think *another precious memory down the drain*. My primary-school friend Megan Bennett also once threw a cricket ball in my face at full speed, something she swears to this day was an accident but I suspect was merely revenge for scribbling on her Puffin Club membership certificate. Perhaps that's responsible too. Bit by bit I am erasing all the elements of my past that make up my story. By the time I am eighty I'll have nothing left but *New Weekly* crossword clues and a habit of politely asking people if they perhaps know what my name might be.

I sense a future where I'm perched at one of those bus stops they set up at old people's homes so Alzheimers sufferers have a hobby outside of smearing their bedroom walls with shit and calling their daughter 'Douglas'. Far from being worrying, I find something intensely comforting about the prospect. What happens when you are wrapped up in the space where memory can no longer reach you? Does it feel safe and blank and fuzzy like that moment where a Valium kicks in and everything around you turns to dust?

Susan tells me she remembers a time, not long after high school, where she hadn't heard from me for a while and called up wanting to say hello.

'And you wouldn't speak to me. You told me you didn't want to be friends anymore. And I just wanted . . . well, I guess I just wanted to know why,' she asks quietly. 'I know it sounds dumb, but it's been sitting with me for all this time. Did I do something wrong?'

Horrified doesn't even come close. She is speaking of a significant moment in our friendship—the *end* of our friendship—and I can't remember. I have no idea what she's talking about. I have coloured that moment of our past over with vague ideas of separate high schools and growing apart. I have reinvented our demise to suit my nefarious purposes. Worst of all, I have attempted to absolve myself of any responsibility over callously hurting the feelings of someone I once adored.

'Oh *that*,' I try out, laughing shakily. 'Really? That was . . . god, it was so long ago.'

'I know. It was just so . . . sudden. I thought I must have done something terrible to make you so upset.'

'No no no no,' I insist. 'It was nothing like that.'

'Then what?'

I pause. What would be worse? Making something up? Or telling her that I'd thoughtlessly erased the entire episode and was sorry she'd wasted so much time worrying about it?

'I'm . . . kind of in the middle of something at work right now,' I lie. 'Can I give you a call back?'

I don't ever phone Susan back. I do exactly as I did to her in 1988 and disappear into the ether. The shame is too great. This petulant, self-absorbed slice of time I carelessly flung away has remained with her for twenty years. I feel like a war criminal, a thief. I think of her, happy with children and occasionally puzzling over why I never responded to her plea for help.

I'm hoping you may be able to solve one of the greatest mysteries of my lifetime so far.

Her friend request is still lingering on Facebook. I am too bitterly ashamed to befriend her, and too laden with guilt to turn her away. After a small amount of detective work I find Joey Dee on Facebook too. He looks old and happy and is still making music. His Myspace page showcases him singing a cover of Marvin Gaye's 'Sexual Healing'.

I'm so sorry, Susan. I wanted to solve your mystery. But

I have too many of my own. There's something wrong with my memory. I'm sorry, Susan. I'm sorry.

• • •

From: ****@bigpond.com
Subject: Re: Okay, so
Date: 20 November 2010 4:23:58 PM
To: Marieke Hardy

Oh Marieke,
I love all the memories, even the ones we'd rather forget (despite the gist of the piece).

I'm not sure which bits are part of your poetic licence . . . I mean, you don't really feel that bad, do you? I would hate to think that you have felt so poorly.

Was I sad when we went our separate ways? Yes. Did I hate you for it? No, not at all. I knew in my heart that I hadn't done anything wrong. I guessed that it was simply the way life goes. High school happens. People grow and change.

If it makes you feel any better, I too turned my back on someone I loved at a poignant time in my life . . . It's a coping mechanism with bad ethics.

All in all, I thank you for responding so honestly. It's more than I could have hoped for. Now go and accept the bloody friend request and be done with it!
You can see my cherub and I'll see God knows what!!
Take care old friend,
Suddenly Sincerely Sue

Down the hatch

It was a letter forwarded on from the kindly folk at the ABC, the address of the book show crossed out (several times, by the looks of things, as though the envelope had bothered varying departments before finding its way to Brunswick) and mine eventually added. PLEASE FORWARD TO. No return address. But the loopy scrawl commanding my attention, shouting my name in biro, should have been a warning. If penmanship were given names like fonts, this one would have been called Lunatic 2.0.

There should be a sticker placed on the correspondence of all lunatics. *Open with caution*, it might read. *Contents may include one or all of the following: 1. Death threat. 2. Question regarding validity of parentage. 3. Kind suggestion that if you don't 'like' a particular subject you 'go back' to 'where you came from', or 4. Faeces*. On the internet it is possible to politely sidestep the hate-fuelled rantings of people who would rather see you dead. A website entitled 'Marieke Hardy Has a Face Like a Big Cunt.net.au' is a title that may ring vague alarm bells, as is anything run by the Westboro Baptist Church. If you don't wish to read a dissertation on why your prose once made someone castrate themselves, don't seek it out. In the case of those more brash among the online community who '@' you directly on Twitter—the equivalent of drunkenly shirt-fronting somebody at a party and screaming 'AND I DON'T MUCH CARE FOR YOUR TIE EITHER'—there's still a 'block user' function. In short: for the most part, it's possible to go about your life happily ignorant that many people in the world think you are a douchebag.

As I opened the letter, a pamphlet fell from the envelope and onto the floor. I ignored it for the moment.

The letter began:

Miss Hardy.

It was a pompous, knowing start, addressing me as though I were a schoolgirl staring down at my scuffed Bata Scouts and regretting that blissful previous hour exchanging saliva with Scott Webster in the toilet block.

I have been watching you on the television for months now and have come to one obvious conclusion. There is a consistency in the subject matter you discuss on the First Tuesday Book Club and if your co-presenters Jennifer Byrne and Jason Steger are too afraid to tell you, I am not. You have the eyes and demeanour of a professional alcoholic. The first step is admitting you have a problem and, Marieke Hardy, as a regular viewer of the show I must inform you IT IS TIME FOR YOU TO TAKE THAT STEP.

I picked up the pamphlet that had fallen to the floor. It was for AA.

This was somewhat of a blow, like being told 'you're not fooling anyone with that stupid haircut, you know. We can still see your forehead.' I chewed the thought over for a moment, feeling it in my mouth.

A complete stranger thinks I am a drunk.

It was no more odd than a complete stranger thinking I was a Communist or a lesbian, both charges having been laid against me in previous unrelated missives from other friendly neighbourhood lunatics. Once I had seen a severely anorexic girl at the Fitzroy pool. All eyes were upon her as she strolled around, glass-cut clavicle jutting from her bathers. I wanted desperately to gently take her aside and point out that people weren't whispering about her because she was glamorous. They were whispering because they were worried about her. Because she looked obviously sick. Because she wasn't hiding her demons like the rest of us were, under the veneer of behaving like functioning human beings.

I wondered for a moment if I was the girl at the Fitzroy pool and my lunatic friend with the loopy writing was me. This thought was soon easily dismissed as I read further and saw his closing paragraph regarding the digital signal of the ABC News 24 channel trying to eat his brain. He was, as originally suspected, a nutjob. My secret life as a heavy drinker could continue unabated.

It's not overtly fashionable, particularly flying in the face of all those startling commercials where unfortunate lads and lasses imbibe one too many alcopops and crash spectacularly through a variety of glass objects, but I really am a huge fan of drinking. I like thinking about it, I like listening to songs about it, and I like reading about it.

If my life of drinking was ever charted for the purposes of medical science it would look as follows: one big pointy triangle for the teenage years of rocket fuel and vomit, a gentle downward slope for the late teens and early twenties, and then an upwards trajectory around the mid-twenties which plateaus, a steady-as-she-goes prairie plain, for over ten years. Moving from a mid-twenties drunk into a mid-thirties drunk is a career choice not everybody likes to make. If you are friends with musicians the line between hedonism and problem drinking is blurred, probably because you are drunk and can't focus properly. You surround yourself with drunks, you read their writing, you fall in love with them. Nobody grows up thinking they're going to be drawn to the one man in the room slouched on a barstool spilling gin on his waistcoat, it just happens. One day you're kissing posters of Pseudo Echo before you go to bed, the next you're piggybacking your boyfriend out of Yah-Yah's at 4 am pleading with him to please stop calling the DJ 'donkey cock' as it's only causing grief.

My illustrious career with the bottle began with the person my mother used to refer to somewhat hopefully as 'your naughty friend', Lisa Jenkins, implying that without Lisa's influence I would probably have spent my downtime cross-stitching and nursing sick orphans. In my mother's mind, Lisa led me astray, beckoning wickedly from the dark corners of teenage immorality. In truth, we were as dangerously unhinged as each other and would spend various evenings placing ourselves in the sort of situations usually re-enacted on *Crime Stoppers* prior to the sobering sentence 'and young Margaret's body was sadly never found'. Lisa's room was on the second storey of her parents' house, so her nightly escapes involved a high-tech rope and pulley system. We encouraged each other dreadfully, comrades in pre-pubescent debauchery. We lost our virginities around the same time to older boys and were frequently separated on school camps 'for the benefit of all concerned'.

Lisa had a penchant for trouble, and liquor, and was possessed of the sort of cockeyed grin usually found on pickpockets, or 1980s Hollywood bad boys the Brat Pack. Her hands were rough and papery. We babysat the children of her neighbours and hunted out their booze and pornography like bloodhounds. We were obsessed with pornography, which was fairly common for private schoolgirls at the age of thirteen if St Trinian's is anything to go by. My great aunt had died five years earlier and left to my family her vast collection of books, at least five of which were intensely pornographic. They were hidden—badly—on the top shelf, amongst Kitty Kelley biographies and *There Goes Whatsisname: The memoirs of Noel Ferrier*. One of my favourites involved a young lass who should probably have known better getting involved with a circus troupe and spending the ensuing one hundred and seventy pages being ravished by midgets and bearded ladies.

Lisa and I were deeply titillated by this, and decided to write an erotic novel of our own. Considering the only significant thing we did outside of school hours was ride the bus, we called it *Sex Bus*. The plot involved a number of hapless commuters boarding without adequate fare or concession card and having to pay their way with sexual favours. Since neither Lisa nor I had been penetrated at that point, most of the sex involved vague descriptions like 'then he did her up the fanny' and 'his ralph stood to attention', the latter of which we had directly copied from Judy Blume's *Forever*. We photocopied *Sex Bus* and handed it out to wide-eyed year sevens on the Balwyn line, an act that these days would likely have us arrested for child pornography. *Sex Bus* grew so popular with a particular group of year nine boys we had to run a reprint in the library, which was a huge career achievement at that point.

Lisa's alcoholic specialty was a potent rocket fuel she concocted from 'anything my parents won't miss from the liquor cabinet'. Since the overwhelming aroma was aniseed there was a fair chance her mother and father weren't huge fans of Sambuca. She would mix and measure with the dexterity of a mad scientist, pouring the final product into a Big Red tomato sauce bottle that I'm fairly certain hadn't been rinsed properly. The end result was something that tasted like a combination of licorice, ketchup, petrol and AIDS. We drank it with gusto.

As a teenager there is no finer way to spend an evening than sitting in a local park taking delicate sips from a tomato sauce bottle and then vomiting into the lap of school heart-throb Stephen Lord, which presumably is why I partook in such activities more often than was healthy. With whispers Lisa and I would steal away from our homes and climb into waiting taxis, picking up helpless boys from Box Hill and Balwyn, Camberwell and Kew. Our lips would be sticky with liqueur. I tapped on more dark bedroom windows than I'd care to remember, swaying unsteadily in the moonlit drive-way and waiting for Stephen or Ashley or Harvey or Clinton to slide out, one Stussy-clad leg after the other. There was no sex, not right away, just hours of whirling, gravity-free gloriousness, the freedom that came with another potent sip.

My first real hangover came courtesy of naughty Lisa Jenkins, too. Another night on rocket fuel, some park or other, some party, some hot, strange, illicit kisses with a boy from the rowing squad up against a dirty wall. It was the night before my family was due to go on an overseas trip and I climbed back into my bedroom window with a head full of slosh and the kind of rolling seasickness common to passengers on the Manly ferry. I made it to the bathroom—just—though the toilet itself seemed infuriatingly out of reach, so I simply vomited a lush combination of spaghetti and rocket fuel all over the floor. Mindful that my still sleep-ing parents weren't to know of my nocturnal activities,

I mopped the whole revolting mess up with tissues, emitting pained little sobs throughout. In photographs from that first day of travel I am with my family, sitting at a New Zealand airport, face the colour of asphalt. There is dried spaghetti on my t-shirt. I look, fittingly, like a teenage drunk.

As I grew older I fell in love with a variety of alcoholics, including Joel, who would carry a 'traveller' at all times in a paper bag. I would open my front door and see him standing there, fresh off the Nicholson Street tram, holding a longneck of beer in one hand and a plastic shopping bag with books and toiletries in it in the other. He looked like a hobo who had just wandered off the street trying to bum loose change. If we went away to the country for the weekend and there was limited access to alcohol, he would panic. On the rare occasions he was sober he couldn't sleep and would just sit at the window and cry quietly, trying not to wake me.

He was a puzzle; a brilliant, acerbic mind consistently seeking oblivion. I tried to keep up with his drinking for a while but in the end there seemed a chasm between us: he had one foot in the camp of serious alcoholics and I saw myself as a visitor. I couldn't understand why he was so insistent on wiping himself out, night after night. I dictated a more moderate drinking routine to him and he told me in no uncertain terms to fuck off. When it was over I said 'we broke up because Joel drank too much' and more often than not had a glass of wine in my hand at the time.

After that I dated every type of alcoholic. Nobody with

a thirst was safe from my affections. Angry brooders, swaggering shot-drinkers, party animals with a bottle of vodka in one arm and naked flame in the other. I remember years ago seeing the breathtakingly clever stand-up comedian Anthony Morgan—himself an excessive drinker—at that very show gulping from a large pint glass of something that quite clearly wasn't water, pacing the stage angrily, veering from the safety of his pre-written routine to launch a tirade against his ex-wife, who had only recently left him for another man.

'He's not even a *proper* alcoholic,' spat Morgan in disgust. 'He's just a *binge drinker*.'

In my late twenties I stayed in a long-term relationship with an alcoholic for three-and-a-half years and we drank the world dry. We drank our way across London, Paris, Barcelona, Tasmania, Far North Queensland and Bali. Every day we would stumble from our beds and wait until the time came when it was reasonable to begin drinking. On holidays, this moment came at around midday. We didn't see ourselves as serious drunks since we didn't drink at breakfast time, except of course in the case of serious code red hangovers when we immediately reached for a bloody mary before even opening our eyes.

For the most part it was a perfectly loving and functional relationship until I began enjoying the odd day sober and he began enjoying the odd day drinking at 10:30 or 11 am. I encouraged him gently to do as I did, step off the treadmill for a fortnight or a week, or even a day, but he seemed completely unable. It came as a shock and with no small amount of sadness the moment I understood that at that point he loved the drink more than he was able to love me.

Alcohol was a perfect mistress who had led me merrily through twenty years of licentiousness and romance, but I didn't think I loved it more than *people*. I wanted to delicately tiptoe that line, to maintain the lifestyle to which I had become accustomed, one hand wrapped around the bottle, the other around a pen. I wanted to be, in other words, a functioning drunk.

I never had a favourite kind of drinker—alcoholics were like children, it was difficult to pick one more special than another and as a fun party trick they too tended to wet themselves when left to their own devices—I just loved men who drank. I still do. There is something deeply untrustworthy about teetotallers, something that emits an aroma of *giving up*. 'I never trust a fighting man who doesn't smoke or drink,' Admiral William Frederick Halsey Jr once said, when enjoying time off from being an outrageous racist. ('Before we're through with them, the Japanese language will be spoken only in hell' was another of his lively conversational kick-starters.) Teetotallers tsk beneath their breath when you reach across to fill up another glass; teetotallers leave parties early. In their eyes is reflected the judgement you are supposed to have fostered for yourself many years ago—that innate responsibility of knowing when to stop and when to say no. Why is that idea in itself so artless? I imagine Jim Morrison peeling away his piss-soaked leathers and taking up jogging and am nearly sick into my mouth. We want our creative icons staggering and helpless with intoxicants. We gravitate towards lovers with dangerous, sharp edges. In the process, we drink to keep up.

When we date, we date drinkers. There is no negotiation to be entered into. Not long ago, I shamelessly asked after a shy tattooed vegan boy who works in a local café and was despondent when I discovered he had subscribed to the strict world of straight-edge. 'He doesn't *drink*,' I sighed miserably, as though this ruled him out from ever being a viable romantic option. If he didn't drink then we couldn't cheat our way through the awkwardness of courtship, couldn't write ourselves off in order to gather the courage to go to bed together. Couldn't spend a weekend away running rampant in a bed and breakfast with a bottle of red. Couldn't get shickered at a friend's wedding and cry on each other in the middle of the dancefloor. There was no point, really, starting anything in the first place. My favourite boyfriends drank and I drank with them and the idea of dating somebody without the comforting 'go on then' nudge of liquor was simply absurd.

As friends grew older there was a polite bowing out of the heavy drinking game. As though they had reached the age of thirty-five and been handed a little pass. *Thanks for drinking with us!* it read. *Enjoy the rest of your life with white wine spritzers and the occasional low-carb beer at family barbecues! Lots of love, your Libertine Youth. P.S. Please don't visit, it only upsets the children.*

They feared, of course, everything we'd read about, everything we'd been told a life of heavy drinking would lead to. Apparently when Hemingway was near the end it was possible to see the outline of his distended and diseased liver lying under the surface of his skin. Is this what will eventually happen to those of us who remain committed, who don't simply murmur 'no thank you, I'm driving' but rather end each and every family get together with dress defiantly held above head and middle finger raised at our cluckingly disapproving GPs? What happens if that dedication to a life lived blurrily doesn't simply continue in carefree afternoons and nights but leads us, helplessly, into a whirlwind of catheters and assisted bathing? That doesn't pique my interest at all. I want to be a pretty drunk, like Dusty Springfield. I want to reach languorously for a margarita while a calypso band lulls me into an afternoon haze. No malfunctioning kidneys just yet, please, no brain haemorrhages. Just the odd hangover that feels like eighty power lifters trying to ejaculate inside your skull all at once.

It's those exact hangovers, of course, which prove to be the breaking point for so many. One day in my early thirties I woke up and stood, naked, in my living room, trying to remember where it was I'd left my car the night before, whilst simultaneously hoping against hope I'd at least had some clothes on when I arrived home. My brain, as it processed this, felt like a cardboard box filled with crumpled newspaper. Then the newspaper caught fire. Then some dwarves appeared out of nowhere attempting to put the fire out. They were naked too. I felt all this frantic activity taking place inside my brain and simply stood helplessly, arms dangling by my side, waiting for it to subside. This was a hangover in your thirties, I told myself. This was different to those days of springing out of bed in your twenties with a mild headache and eating a banana sandwich. This is where you could actually feel those important little puzzle pieces of your brain melt away.

There haven't been blackouts. Not too many. A delicate handful. What's a few blackouts between friends? Yet the older I got the more colourful they seemed to become. At twenty-eight I collapsed unconscious on a stranger's lawn. At thirty-three, after a night spent on a friend's rooftop in Sydney doing shots, I crawled into his bedroom and passed out. I woke up, fascinatingly, in the bedroom of a completely different member of the house, a gay man named Peter. Apparently I had walked into his room at 5am nude and looking, in his words, 'like the girl from *The Ring*'. With nary a second thought I had climbed into his bed and curled into a ball and gone to sleep. His first thought was 'holy mother of christ'. His second: 'girls are soft'. His third: 'I am getting the hell out of this bed with this drunk naked madwoman and going upstairs to sleep on the couch.' To this day I am simply grateful that I didn't do a wee in the corner of his bedroom. Perhaps I did and Peter had just been too polite to tell me.

There is apparently something even more shameful in this sort of behaviour for women. Women aren't supposed to drink heavily or write about it unless they've left it behind, in a cane basket full of old hurts and solved problems. There is a neatness in moving on from a past of heavy drinking for women, a sad and brave memoir full of tales of regret. Caroline Knapp writes well about being a drunk in her novel *Drinking: A love story*, but the book ends with lots of therapy and hugging and misty-eyed talk about facing a new dawn sober. The best writing about drinking is masculine writing, inebriated writing. Why? And when will women challenge HL Mencken's assertion that 'The harsh, useful things of the world, from pulling teeth to digging potatoes, are best done by men who are as starkly sober as so many convicts in the death-house, but the lovely and useless things, the charming and exhilarating things, are best done by men with, as the phrase is, a few sheets in the wind'?

It's time for women to romanticise drinking. Forget brushing off the indignities contained in a bottle of Drambuie, or carrying on with lives making babies and pretending we were never once the author of a three-page poem entitled 'The revolution begins at the bottom of my West Coast Cooler'. Why can we not too lay claim to the brutish gorgeousness of falling asleep on the 'j' key of a laptop? I know plenty of salty ladies who come undone at the thought of a whisky sour and an evening spent whirling around dens of ill repute, sticky with devilish thoughts and tobacco smoke. So where is the woman who writes the equivalent of Charles Bukowski's 'Drinking is an emotional thing. It joggles you out of the standardism of everyday life, out of everything being the same. It yanks you out of your body and your mind and throws you against the wall. I have the feeling that drinking is a form of suicide where you're allowed to return to life and begin all over the next day. It's like killing yourself, and then you're reborn. I guess I've lived about ten or fifteen thousand lives now'? Perhaps they're afraid that one too many feature articles in *Imbibers Monthly* will lead to a swathe of letters from helpful members of the community. ('The first step, Anaïs, is admitting you have a problem.')

The trick is to admire the artistic outpourings of other drunks from a safe distance without fear of living out the rest of your days face first in a bowl of peanuts right next to Norm in the *Cheers* bar. Listen to Donald Newlove, a man who was so enamoured with the combination of alcohol and prose he wrote a book entitled *Those Drinking Days: Myself and other writers*. When Newlove writes about being drunk in the novel's first half, it is in homage: 'I patiently uncurled the English tongue to make it speak plain but it kept tying itself into gorgeous knots I couldn't make sense of. And if the knot had a hard glow, like sunlight on snow, then I didn't care about sense. This light overrode sense, or the need for it. Light is all. This, I'd assure myself with a thankful glance toward heaven, this is the best prose I've ever written.'

I want to marry writing like that. I want to put it in a brandy snifter and set fire to it. I want to smash a bottle against it and ride it out to sea. Yet Newlove then renounces drinking in the second half of his book and pens instead many glowing paragraphs about how improved his life is since he's stopped punching random publishers in the face and wearing his stained purple suit on first dates. *Those Drinking Days* becomes, in that moment, an infinitely dull read. I believe I actually muttered the word 'quitter' aloud when closing the book.

In the face of all the negative press, all the po-faced *body+soul* liftouts promoting AFDs and clean living and shiny, brand-new livers, it is more than admirable that there are those promoting a louche life lived underground. Fuck sobriety, they say. Let us mingle for a few more precious moments in the half-light of gin's muse. Let us celebrate the temporary relief of tuning out. Let us love harder and burn brighter.

Kingsley Amis put it beautifully when he wrote:

> The reason why I, and most others, usually turn out to enjoy meeting such creatures is simply and obviously the co-presence of drink. The human race has not devised any way of dissolving barriers, getting to know the other chap fast, breaking the ice, that is one-tenth as handy and efficient as letting you and the other chap, or chaps, cease to be totally sober at about the same rate in agreeable surroundings. Well and good, the serious student of the effects of drink will retort in the grim, curmudgeonly tone peculiar to serious students of the effects of drink; well and good, but what about what happens later? What about those who drink, not to cease to be totally sober, but to get drunk? What about the man who *drinks on his own*? . . . Leaving aside dipsomaniacs, most or many of whom are born, not made, I feel that there is very little we can safely add, in discussing our motives for drinking, to the verdict of the poet who said we do it because

'we are dry, or lest we may be by and by, or any other reason why'.

Of course, KA was a fat old pomp who saw women as a bothersome arrangement of piffle and noise and died desperately lonely, but that's neither here nor there. He's correct, drinking alone is somehow seen as something disgraceful. 'I drink,' friends say to me with a self-effacing superiority, 'but I don't drink alone.' I can't see the issue with this. Drinking alone is often infinitely preferable to drinking with others. For one thing, you don't have to tolerate the company of other drunks. You don't have to notice the moment they first slur their words, indicating the beginning of the end of the night, the sorry moment a once enjoyable conversation slides muddily into an overloud self-congratulatory circle of wank. If you drink alone you can prank call ex-lovers, listen to Toots and the Maytals with the volume turned up so loud your neighbour calls the police, and go on Chatroulette with complete strangers whilst wearing only your underpants and a Ronald Reagan mask.

Drinking alone is life affirming and a joyous exercise. I do it because sometimes I am simply jack of toeing the line and being good and I want to give myself over to the rakish unpredictability that liquor offers. And for that I'm willing to stand up and be counted, to not write a sad and breathy memoir about bar-hopping days of yore or tip out all my Campari bottles in martyrish ritual. This one's for the drinking girls.

I will file that lunatic's letter and its accusatory pamphlet away, along with the aerogramme telling me I dress like a common prostitute, and the postcard helpfully pointing out that my forehead is too big for my face and if I am in any way set on a further career in the public eye I should have it seen to. I'm aware these kind people are only trying to assist me, but so far I have made a life out of being a drunk with the sort of forehead you could project 3D movies on and if it's all the same to them I'll carry on doing so and sifting through matters in my own sweet time. There may have to come a day when I put down the wine glass. I know that. But everything until then is fluid. Everything until then is liquid.

Parts of this story first appeared in Frankie *magazine.*

The Bubble

We were known as the Bubble.

It was a name that sprang, I suppose, from the all-pervasive bubble of fun that surrounded us at all times. Nobody could remember who coined it. It probably started one morning as we sat on some sagging rooftop, eyes curly-wurly with sleeplessness and chemicals, watching a *Miami Vice* pink dawn break across Melbourne. We were sprawled out over each other, half covered in blankets, clothes askew. Somebody spoke in hazy murmur.

'I think I'm supposed to go to work today.'

There was a collective outcry at this, a chorus of sleepy condemnation. Nobody should have to work today. Not today, not any day. Nobody should have to leave this rooftop, ever. We should just stay up here forever and demand somebody fetch cocktails for us and while out the remainder of our days being young and handsome and on a roof and off our faces. It would be groundbreaking.

'Just *stay*.'

'I know, I should. I don't want to leave the bubble.'

It was the Bubble then, officially, with a capital 'B', and remained thus for about three years. There were twelve of us, musicians and lovers and furniture makers, as well as a handful of addendums who would come along for a four or five month ride, holding on for dear life in their side-cart as we powered forward, demolishing everything in our path. Those inside floated about like dust. Being ensconced in the Bubble represented being free of responsibility, of commitment. There were never any emotional repercussions to dreadful behaviour. You could get away with just about anything and somebody else in the Bubble would inevitably have your back. There was simply safety. The next soiree. Forget about the trouble and strife. Let's open another bottle of champagne.

Parties would go for two days and in a groaning heap we would collapse in the Edinburgh Gardens with six packs of beer and olives from Piedmontes. At home waiting for us would be unanswered emails and telephone messages from irate parents and, on some occasions, a partner in floods of tears wondering why the fuck the other side of the bed hadn't been slept in for a fortnight. Rather than face this melee, we would simply stay in the Bubble. Turn the mobile phones off. Pretend everything in the outside world was simply an illusion, designed to test our will. Somebody would suggest we head to the Builder's Arms to see The Forefathers play. After that we could go to Alia for booty night and dance to Jay-Z like the busted-up kids we were. We would crash out on each other's couches, floors, beanbags, soggy with substances, and wake up and do it all again. Breakfast at the Tin Pot. Afternoon wines in the backyard. Another two-day party.

The Bubble had a secret language, an impenetrable dictionary full of in-jokes and songs and nicknames and lewd tales. We played Gin Rummy and the Italian card game Scopa with shrieks and slaps and our own set of rules. There was a vaguely abhorrent period where we chanted every time we were in public. We took Polaroid photographs of each other and stuck them to toilet walls.

In retrospect we were probably the most obnoxious people in the universe. But in your twenties being in the Bubble was the sort of thing that kept you breathing.

Everybody is, at that age, a refugee from another friendship group, another time. We somehow fell in with each other, an unspoken contract in unspilt blood. It never seemed to be a choice. It was accepted as fate.

Two of the boys in the Bubble played in Dallas Crane and it was the done thing to show up at every gig, waving beers in the air and singing along to all the songs. After one week-long party refused to end, I clambered into a stranger's van and followed them up to the Broadford Bike Bonanza. Enormous bearded men in leather vests howled at the moon. There were fires, women who spat. The echoed revving of powerful engines, mating calls of a desert wolf. The band took to the stage, all skinny denim and zip-up Beatle boots from Roccos. They looked, in the eyes of their hard-bitten audience, like flamboyant homosexuals, possibly five minutes away from bursting into an upbeat rendition of 'YMCA'. Pat, the bass player, instantly started to regret wearing white pants. His party trick involved falling asleep before anybody else. We called it 'Bernie-ing out' because once he was unconscious we acted like he was the lead role in *Weekend at Bernie's* and took photos of him doing things like eating cigarette butts and sticking his finger up Dirty Derek's arse.

Someone threw a tinny at the stage. Someone else threw a spider. A *spider*? I could see the look on Shannon's face. He turned to me in confusion and panic, shrinking behind the drum kit.

'Someone threw a *spider*,' he mouthed.

I didn't really think before I stripped off. It was an oddly auspicious occasion where I just happened to be wearing matching underwear. Dallas Crane played a very loud rock 'n' roll song. I ran on with them and jumped around like an idiot only recently released from an asylum. I had been awake at that point for three days and would stay awake for at least a couple more. People stopped throwing spiders. Maybe there were no spiders in the first place.

Dallas Crane were essentially the focal point of the Bubble. If they were playing somewhere it was an unspoken meeting place; somewhere you would go and know without question half the people at the bar. Ted Danson was right, sometimes you want to go where everybody knows your name. None of us would think twice about following the band to Ballarat and watching them play a show, or spending eight hours at the Espy from soundcheck to last drinks. We would help carry out Shan's drum kit to his mincy-looking

Vanette, hoisting the snare above our heads and weaving about in the car park. At an after party in Collingwood the lead singer—the Denim Sausage, an ex-boyfriend of mine once savagely referred to him as—spent the night cowering in fear in a bedroom while his girlfriend raged through the house trying to hunt him down. I wish I'd seen him climb out through the front window and onto Sackville Street to make his escape. It must have looked like Meatloaf trying to flee from a mineshaft. You couldn't blame him, though. Dave was on the run from reality like the rest of us.

Four little boys used to come to every Dallas Crane show too, crammed down the front of the stage, whooping and hollering and gazing up at the band with open-mouthed expressions of adoration. They formed a band themselves eventually, and called it Jet. We watched from the sidelines, graceless and sore as hell, as their startling career trajectory took them in what seemed a matter of minutes from Tuesday night gigs at the Duke of Windsor to the life of international superstars. They played the Fuji rock festival and supported the Rolling Stones. When one of them bought a summer home on Lake Como we set to badmouthing him so hard it's a wonder his ears didn't turn to ash.

Everybody in the Bubble lazily slept with everybody else. It was gluttonously sexual. Too young for the Grim Reaper commercials to have any real impact, we indulged in promiscuity with fervour. I had begun to fall in love with Sime while he was half dating somebody else. We tried to have serious conversations about love in the backyard on overcast mornings. A pair of apostrophes on the concrete, coffee in hand.

'Do you think I'm a hussy?'

It was laughable. We were all hussies. It was why we got along so famously, probably.

'I hope not,' I said, 'because that cheapens whatever this is with you and me. And I don't think it's cheap.'

'Cheap, no. Confusing, yes,' he replied, pulling his trucker's cap down over his eyes.

Women were hitting him over the head with things at that stage. At parties he would face infuriated ex-girlfriends with violence in their eyes. Ice-cube trays and blocks of wood. He was having a bad run. We decided on a whim, somewhere in the midst of that perfect entropy, to have a pine forest wedding. The Bubble stood around us and threw confetti and for a while at least he escaped the routine of being smacked around by past lovers. I loved him as much as I was capable of then, which was with everything I had left after devoting every inch of my waking life to my friends. He was subsumed into the Bubble and acquiesced gracefully. We barely paused to take a breath for long enough to sign the marriage licence.

It was probably the fog of acceptance that allowed that glorious period of The Bubble to stretch out for so long, a morally ambiguous vacation without calendar or close. The more time we spent together the more people had trouble telling us apart, as though we were just a braying mass of arms and legs and joy and flesh.

Gabi and I, being of similar build, being dark, being fond of neckerchiefs, would often be mistaken for the other. We didn't discourage the confusion. I would titter graciously when complimented on my spastic burlesque dancing, she would grin bashfully when congratulated on her work with *The Age*. We tried to have a threeway once ('wouldn't that be a *scream*'), in a bedroom beaded with sweat above an Indian restaurant. Outside the room, a party throbbed. We kept seeing ourselves reflected in the eyes of the other and ended up laughing so hard we couldn't go on, much to the obvious displeasure of our rapidly deflating contender.

On mornings after we would drag ourselves from sleep, heads rattling like dice, and look in dismay at our to-do list. There were family lunches to go to. A work meeting. Some breeder was holding a baby shower.

'We can't just say we're hungover and can't make it,' Gabi once lamented. 'It's not a decent enough excuse.'

'We need another excuse, then. Something they can't argue with.'

'Just strange them out. Invent a really messed up reason.'

'Fine.'

Which is how, I guess, we once texted a girlfriend with apologies regarding her afternoon tea party.

Dog shat bed, the text read. *Not coming*.

We bought a bottle of wine and a wheel of white Castello cheese and sat in the backyard squirting each other with Super Soakers. Everybody came over and told us we'd done the right thing by not going. We were staying in the Bubble.

The Bubble put on an art show. We drew names out of hats and created a secret art piece based on another member of the group. For weeks everybody worked tirelessly, sheathed in giggles and whispers. Upstairs at a bar on Smith Street, we showed off the results of our labours and congratulated ourselves on our cleverness and unshakeable friendship. It couldn't have been more self-absorbed and beautiful. 'Look at us,' we were saying. 'Look at how much we love each other. Look at how funny and interesting and devoted we are. This can never change. This will never change.' Dirty Derek made stickers featuring a wicked looking child holding a big ball up to his face. SMELL THE BUBBLE, it said, with details of the exhibition printed beneath. 'Everybody is showing tonight.'

It never felt exclusive but people inevitably started feeling left out. The high fashion Fitzroyals despised our pack mentality and one of them kicked a window in at the gallery on the exhibition's opening night. Drunk, we suggested a street duel, like in *West Side Story*, to be held on Johnston Street. Them in their Lush wide-legged pants and asymmetrical haircuts, us in Miller shirts and cowboy boots. Last person left dancing gets dibs on the Napier Hotel. They took one look at us, boorish and ridiculous, and walked away.

'The Napier is ours!' cried Spicer, in skittish triumph.

The Bubble used to make an annual visit to Lake Eildon, where we would hire out houseboats and spend the weekend cheating death by writing ourselves off and racing speedboats in the nude. We weren't allowed to commandeer a speedboat without a licenced driver, so Blair simply went and got his licence on the morning of the trip. He was nicknamed 'GTD' with good reason. He didn't get a question wrong in the exam, just walked out grinning and waving his new boat licence over his head. We made him personalised business cards to celebrate. Gold, with a cartoon of his capable face gracing one side. 'Get Things Done' it read simply, with his mobile number beneath.

The houseboat trips were exercises in heedlessness. Cath's sister broke her leg in two places and was forced to sit on the back of the boat in abject agony while eight people high on drugs told her not to worry, it was probably just a scratch, here, have some Panadeine Forte and a red wine. Her face was etched with pain and the Panadeine Forte pulsated through her bloodstream and made her vomit. Dirty Derek, who had been watching over her in a fatherly fashion, took one look at the ice cream container full of upchuck and vomited too. Somebody else passing decided all that vomiting seemed a great lark, and heaved lavishly into the water. It was like that scene in *Stand By Me* where the fat kid makes an entire community of rednecks puke. I kept waiting for Richard Dreyfuss's voice to say something pithy and poignant about all that we were going through. In the end the poor girl had to wait til morning, when somebody was finally sober enough to take her into town and ferry her to a doctor. Word trickled back to the boat that she was alive and in plaster and we toasted her health and good fortune.

Inspired by the Eildon surrounds we would strip off and roll around in the mud, feral with drink. I formed an army with Derek and Larkis and we stood for hours in the shallows, naked skin burning, jabbing oversized sticks at anybody who dared attempt to pass. Somebody took a photograph of us from behind, standing there, backsides grazing the water. Dirty Derek ultimately turned it into a painting. You can see it now, hanging over a bar in High Street. At the time, we wanted to document everything. Art shows and videos and paintings and Polaroids. Perhaps even then we knew it wouldn't last forever.

It was on one of those Eildon trips that we saw a light plane dip across the lake. Afterwards, everybody swore they caught the moment it clipped the power lines and fell, but mostly we remembered when all the emergency services vehicles started circling the water. Four people were missing. We watched from the shore as a helicopter buzzed overhead in vain hope of finding life.

'Fuck,' somebody said.

We did not want this reminder of our mortality. You could sense the pull of pain and real life.

Jarrod opened another beer and we turned our backs to the water.

'How did we not die?' I said to Blair, years later. 'All that riding around in the speedboat . . . everybody was so fucked up.'

'I don't know. We just didn't.'

'Yes, but *how*?'

After the crash I started leaving parties early, tasting the hangover even before I'd taken my first drink. That front-row ticket to death had shaken me. I became famous for my sneak-away act, perfecting the art of being mid-conversation with somebody and then disappearing as they turned to refill their drink. 'The Hardy Slip-Off', the Bubble would call it, annoyed by my cunning. I hated goodbyes at parties, hated once I'd decided to leave being strongarmed into staying for one more drink, one more pill, one more investment in tomorrow's hangover. If I was caught picking up my bag and sliding out the front door I would lie and say I was just going to the 7-Eleven to buy a mixer, or Pringles. If the person who caught me called my bluff I would be inevitably dragged back into somebody's bedroom or other, where the rest of the party all lay in a big messy pile, and find myself talking about Alex Chilton records until morning.

One time it was Gabi who caught me. She had stepped off the living-room dancefloor for a rare moment and was getting a glass of water. I froze, guiltily, one arm in my dufflecoat.

'You're not *going*.'

'It's five-thirty in the morning!'

Gabi came close. Pointed to the living room. I could hear the delighted rodeo of fun, of a room crammed full of everybody we knew and loved at that moment. Nobody was missing. Everybody was in. All hands on deck.

'All this,' she said solemnly. 'It's not going to last forever.'

'Please don't try and guilt trip me.'

'It *won't*.'

She was right. This permutation of people, the comradely 'all in' mentality, couldn't last. It would break and scatter, little pieces of glass. Somebody would decline a party invitation due to a work function and then someone else would get pregnant and the Bubble would pop. It was bound to happen eventually. At the time, though, it felt endless.

Gabi likes to remind me of this story.

'You took your coat off and ran on to the dancefloor,' she smiles. 'For once you came back. I bet you're glad you did now.'

The Bubble parties grew more debauched, the need to behave in a fashion more brutal and urgent. We would wake up, not remembering coming home, not recalling who we'd been with or what we'd done with them.

Over afternoon drinks recently I was told about a girl who went through a terrifying stage of getting blind drunk and going home with strange men and shitting somewhere mysterious in their houses.

'She'd wake up knowing something terrible had happened,' my friend said solemnly, 'but not know where she'd done it.'

'What sort of places did she shit?'

'Oh, everywhere. Behind the couch or the curtains, mostly. Once she did it on a pile of unwashed dishes in the sink. Then she went to see a psychologist who told her it was a direct result of father issues.'

I found this intensely funny and strange and frightening. And then remembered that one day, in the thick of Bubbledom after a long bender, when Gabi appeared in the doorway of my bedroom.

'You have to see this,' she said with a shocked expression, beckoning me into the bathroom.

Someone had shat in a drawer.

'Did you do this?' I asked her.

She looked horrified.

'No! Of course not. I mean . . .' she paused. We looked into the drawer again. 'I was pretty out of it when I came home. But I think I'd remember . . . *this*.'

We agreed that yes, one would probably recall doing something as significant as rising from bed in the middle of the night and going to the toilet in a drawer full of makeup and hairpieces, which thankfully ruled us both out. We further agreed that it was probably Matty, who was still at this moment passed out in my bedroom and seemed overall capable of such an act. But the fact remained that for a moment we had doubted ourselves. Our brains were so fried with drink and night there was a chance that in the brume of sleep we had stooped that low. Did I really do that?

'And on top of your favourite *scarf*,' I wailed to Gabi

sympathetically, conveniently ignoring the fact that a soiled neckerchief was probably the least of our problems given that we were now getting so fucked up somebody in our house was shitting on furniture.

The unfairness and acceptance of adulthood and responsibility kept creeping upon us, piece by piece. Shannon and his girlfriend Jonesy broke up, then Sime and I did. Gabi and her feller danced a few torturous rounds before she left him for the American guitarist who would become the father of her child. Our Scottish friend Danny, who had led the immigration department on a merry chase for years, was eventually tapped on the shoulder and sternly asked to leave the country. We trooped out to the airport as one to say goodbye, dressed in idiotic costumes, chanting, making a racket. Someone was passing a hipflask full of whisky. Danny kept his split-melon grin for most of the day before it fell apart, in a big mess of wet washing, right at the departure gates. As he waved goodbye, the fare-thee-well smiles faded from our faces too, and the gravity of our loss began to sink in.

He didn't come back for four years.

Eventually everybody started throwing the word 'depression' about like 'drug comedown' or 'period pain'. It was used as an excuse for cheating, for the most part. One untidy night in the toilets at the Tote, when revealed in a blister of finger pointing and recrimination, was credited entirely to depression.

'I'm so sorry I had sex with that bartender in an alley off Little Lonsdale Street,' we pleaded through sobs and curled up, agonised fingers. 'I think . . . I think I have *depression*.'

Depression was the reason we had such long and torturous affairs, sneaking guiltily off to the beige surrounds of the City Crown Hotel while unassuming partners toured the country. Depression was the reason we ingested chemicals and chased tail at music festivals. Depression was the reason I had another three-way which ended in a huge fight complete with hair-pulling and the spat-out, accusing question *why don't you two just stay here and fuck each other then*?

I asked my father about my Great Aunty Mary, who shot herself in the head when I was eight years old. I remember walking to the milk bar with my friend Amanda and seeing the story spread-eagled across the front page of the *Sun*. MARY HARDY SUICIDE.

'Your Aunt Mary ... she was very moody. She drank heavily,' he began. 'She was always surrounded by people, but she was very lonely.'

It was easier to sidestep the potential diagnosis and carry on self-medicating with hard liquor. Who knew if it really was a chemical imbalance, or simply the bleating mantra of a mid-twenties hedonist with no excuses remaining up their sleeve? Nobody had the inclination to see psychologists or GPs back then; we just bandied about the 'D' word as a lazy fallback. Some of us were probably horribly and clinically depressed. Others were just sad the party looked as though it were coming to a close.

As time passed there was a profane amount of crossfading

behind closed doors, sad remnants of each relationship seeping into another. A comforting ear would turn into a comforting bed and before too long most of us would turn up at a party and realise we'd slept with almost everybody in the room. Ex-lovers were growing rightly bitter. Cruelty was never intended, but inevitably people were hurt. I would try to turn away from the angry eyes of an increasing number of ex-partners to seek comfort in the Bubble, but the Bubble wasn't always there. We were beginning to drift apart.

Dallas Crane played their last show. I didn't go. Neither did Gabi.

'They'll play again,' we told ourselves.

They did, only once, when the man they named their band after was struck down with terminal cancer. The gig was a fundraiser to cover medical costs. It seemed a stark and sobering fact: Dallas Crane was dying. Those of us who went stood up the back of the Tote, listening to songs we used to regard as anthems. We looked old and felt foolish. After the show the band barely spoke to each other. Pat and Shannon hung out in the front bar. Dave and Pete locked themselves in the band room.

The Bubble started meeting in reduced numbers, in factions, and the conversation became, over time, less about what we were going to do than what we had once done. We revelled in past glories, in that slice of time when we had been perfect and loved and unencumbered by responsibility. And yet with this acceptance of life outside, we were conceding what we had never done before: that we were just like everybody else. We would have babies and get fat and quit drinking and not spend every waking moment together. We would turn up to events for which we had accepted invitations without texting absurd excuses. We had grown up.

It was an essential part of letting go, deciding which ribbons of the past we wanted to tie around our fingers and which were best left on the maypole.

I could weep for the unfairness of it all now. For the necessity in closing the door on the travelling salesman of youth. I could weep with such fondness for us all.

Born this way

For a few not unlively moments in a Kew hospital in 1976 my father believed I had been born with a penis. Wait, there's more. Not only did he believe I'd been born with a penis, he also believed said penis was so gargantuan it was capable of wrapping itself around my tiny, newborn throat and cutting off my air supply. Which it seemed to be, astoundingly, in the process of doing at that exact second.

'It's a boy!' he exclaimed with a mixture of pride and alarm. 'And *what* a boy!'

I don't know exactly how it all played out after that, which member of the medical team was the first to gently tap him on the arm and explain in hushed tones that the long pink thing turning my face blue was not in fact my genitalia but my umbilical cord and that if he didn't mind quieting down as they attempted to save the life of his newborn daughter it would be most appreciated, but he got the idea eventually and backed into a corner, chastened.

My mother likes to bring this story up at least once a

year. 'Remember the time your father thought you were born with an enormous penis?' she says fondly, while my dad makes a lot of noise about how overblown the whole incident was and anybody might have made the same mistake and isn't it just a blessing she was a healthy baby and so forth.

They were very into 'hands on' parenting, channelling all their energy and enthusiasm for performance into raising their child. As out-of-work actors they rarely had anything better to do with their time than indulge my elaborately imaginative play scenarios. A request for a game of hospitals would involve not only a white coat and stethoscope costume, but a variety of role changes, from consumptive patients ('I think . . . it's fatal,' my mother would gasp, collapsing onto the floor of my bedroom with seemingly uncontrollable tremors) to pacing, concerned GPs. To my father's eternal credit he continued to play these games with me even when I turned into a sniggering, helpless eight year old and named all the patients juvenile things like 'Mrs Cock' or 'The Boobie Twins'.

'Mrs Boobie? I'm afraid it's bad news,' he would announce, stroking his beard, and as the mother of these unfortunate twins I would duly enter a state of deep shock, all the while trying to contain myself at the abject hilarity of my brilliant surname.

My mother loved me with a searing devotion and was always available for my clinging, emotionally overwrought needs, but insists that after I was born she was more determined than ever to be known as something other than 'just a mother'.

'You gave me,' she says, not unkindly, 'a reason to get out of the house and do something else with my life.'

She tap-danced when she was heavily pregnant, an activity she often rudely and publicly states 'explains a great deal', and raised me with a sense of independence and a propensity for cussing at passing drivers and running away from home. From my mother I have learned how to listen to others, how to organise my life with an unnerving rigidity, and to *always* say please and thank you in mixed company lest she somehow appear in the background with a looming glare and vague promise of violence.

We marched into that predictable two-person war, of course, when I became an adolescent and overnight she turned into Hitler. There were four dreadful years when my beleaguered father was forced to creep between the bedrooms of the two women in his family, imploring one to please apologise, and then sheepishly telling the other that he's not exactly sure where her daughter got to but the flyscreen on her window seemed to have been slashed open and her bed not slept in and did she think it was perhaps time to call the police yet or should they give it a few more hours.

This was a time when my mother and I wholly despised each other, when any sign of nurturing on her part would propel me into another burst of juvenile delinquency and her into going down to the local river and hitting herself on the head with rocks or whatever ritual it was grieving mothers of her generation were compelled to undertake during times of crisis. I once bullied her into such a frenzy of rage she actually wrestled me to the ground, much to the horrified shouts of my onlooker pacifist father. Both being on the short and round side we must have appeared to all and sundry like two babushka dolls engaged in a fight to the death, though it didn't feel comedic at the time.

'When?' she would scream as I shoved her off me with all the grace of WWF wrestler Ricky 'The Dragon' Steamboat and raced out the front door to run wild. 'When did you turn into such . . . an *arsehole*?'

Time healed us, created a bridge between the slights and the lies and the mistrust, and we moved as adults into a warmer, more comradely partnership.

She was—and remains—a very good mother; open to any and every discussion, and a proponent of creative, generous living at all times. Though she's never been one of those women described as 'born to parent'. There's an expectation that these delightful nurturing instincts set certain females apart from their sisters, draw a line in the sand of compassion that may rarely be crossed. A propensity for tea parties, a 'way' with dolls, tending to a scabbed-up knee with concerned frowns: these are the character traits of a very pleasant somebody born to make babies. Those failing to similarly measure up are spoken of in mean-spirited, disparaging terms. 'She's not very *motherly*, is she?' remains, as a character appraisal, on a par with 'She takes a while to warm up' and 'I just think she really enjoys the music of Jack Johnson.' Display an iota of awkwardness when playing with a child and you are dismissed, pitied, slotted into the stiff-backed category of Cruella de Vils or wicked stepmother types who would rather skin puppies than do anything so maladroit as nappy changing.

Motherhood fit my best friend Gabi like a glove. She had a big European laugh and squeezed people hard and affectionately on the arm when they were talking to her and everybody I knew was kind of in love with her and that was just fine by me. Gabi had an enormous bosom and the sort of perfect round bottom everybody liked to put an admiring hand on as she walked past, even strangers. If you saw her you would instantly want to rest your face on her chest and tell her your secrets. She was like the walking embodiment of the Tom Waits *Rain Dogs* album cover.

In our twenties we developed a beautiful kind of symmetry. After the insistent passage of skin-graft bonding where we took not a step without permission of the other, the whispered insistence that from now on we should experience each of life's lessons hand-in-hand or not at all, there came a distinct lull in proceedings—a perfect, unbroken calm, where we simply found joy in co-existing and seeing the world through the same set of eyes. And then all of a sudden one of us rather startlingly managed to fertilise an egg and everything that we had known up til that point seemed obsolete. I made coffee. Gabi made babies. The atom had split.

I was living with her and her American partner—a one-man band who toured the world wearing a lycra jumpsuit and a motorcycle helmet with a telephone receiver glued to it—when, out of nowhere, she announced that they were pregnant. It came as somewhat of a shock to all three of us. Certainly, there had been many a wine-soaked conversation about one day moving to the country and starting some sort of ukulele collective with our respective partners and various future children, but that seemed a world away. Gabi was still hiding up the back of rock-fogged gigs, and drinking too much on the weekends, and performing a variety of absurd living room aerobics—Denise Austin-style legwarmers and all—with me as ever by her side. We travelled together, and wept in each other's arms, and collapsed in noisy hysterics in the middle of crowded shopping malls, but most of all we always understood exactly what the other was going through. We empathised and listened and felt. And now she was entering a mystifying world I had scant idea of past archaic copies of *Where Did I Come From?*

I didn't really have any other close girlfriends who had been knocked up. The ones on the burnt edges of my social circle seemed to just drift off into that vaguely terrifying world of afternoon paddle pools and hideous postmodern rock 'n' roll baby tees and were seen again only on the occasional wild night on the tear where they left their offspring in the hands of an understanding relative and hit the town with a vigour that bordered on demonic.

'I am going to get *so fucked up*,' they would announce determinedly, lining up the shots, ignoring the fact that their nipples were leaking through their shirt, and occasionally snapping out of an exhausted, dead-eyed stare to yell 'WOO-HOO' like someone who had awoken from a coma and suddenly found themselves at a baseball game. We would welcome them back into the hedonism fold, asking polite questions about how their anal tearing was healing up, and then watch in silence as they were carried out about five minutes later unconscious and covered in pinot noir.

Obviously I was for the most part thrilled for Gabi. She was a patient, nurturing soul, the gift of mama ran through her blood and she was no doubt going to make some wide-eyed infant blissfully happy. It was more a fear of the unknown that froze me up. I thought that perhaps motherhood would take the spirit of the wicked from her eyes; propel her into making friendlies with other harried, underslept women who had survived that dark night of screaming sobs and leaving me and my paltry concerns about Facebook and snake-hipped guitar players for dust. I was afraid—in the most patently selfish way—of losing her forever. That she would have to, by the decree of nature, love somebody else more than she loved me.

Over the course of nine months she went from being foxy, self-assured '50s bombshell Gabi to foxy, self-assured '50s bombshell Gabi with a massive novelty beach ball shoved up her jumper. She felt vomitous in the kitchen, sighed longingly at brandy shots whilst sticking with soda water, and the requisite amount of months later produced a creature so breathtakingly beautiful we were all awed. She had done it, crossed over, and I could only now make noises of empathy regarding her experiences. When she spoke of Delilah I would nod and attempt to understand, but the innate perception I had once shared with her was missing. Our friendship had become a song without lyrics.

Sometimes, though, I would just sit and admire her endless patience; the way she would explain the concept of chopsticks eight hundred and three times or spend seven hours constructing a baby drum kit which Delilah looked at with contempt before choosing to instead play with a booger she found on the floor which may or may not have originated in her own nose. I pondered how I would do it differently, or how I might attempt to ape her methods if I had my own child.

I had become an inadvertent mother at the age of twenty-four when I fell in love with a man named Sime who had a six-month-old daughter. Both the relationship and the child were unplanned. He and I had been friends for years—had even dated, briefly and shyly, at the ages of twenty-three and nineteen respectively—and spent the majority of our time together since happily introducing our various partners to each other and co-existing in the summery orbit of the mid-1990s Fitzroy music scene. It was a heady time, full of interminable VCA funk bands like Cranky and Dylan Lewis's Brown Hornet who played on Thursday nights at the Evelyn or the Rainbow or the Empress. They all had horn sections and each band member was inexplicably allowed at least one nine-minute solo in every song. These were the sorts of gigs people attended and sat on the floor gazing up at with a dumb intensity, or leaped about in front of the stage as though poked with an electric cattle prod in the name of being a 'free spirit'. We undulated from pub to pub, a mass of high spirits in beanies and vests and the odd misguided terry-towelling three-quarter-length shorts sold at Ministry of Style on Brunswick Street. Sime sang in various bands, beautifully, and spent his downtime making sculpture or working at the Vic Markets. He had big black eyes and corduroy pants and he played the harmonica. Offstage he would sit in dark corners alone rolling cigarettes and staring into space and everybody thought him to be deliciously moody. He began a timorous love affair which produced a child, to the apparent surprise of all involved. They called the baby Edie—a tiny, serious creature with eyes as deep and knowing as her father's. When Sime's relationship with Edie's mother faltered and he found himself temporarily homeless, I suggested in the spirit of friendliness he come and live in the bungalow out the back of my house. One night we both came home drunk and kissed, unexpectedly. 'All bets are off,' Sime said. We kissed again. Fireworks exploded over Melbourne. We guessed that was probably a good sign. Two weeks after that we decided that it was probably worth all the shit we were going to get from our respective ex-partners and that we should leap into a love affair headfirst.

He never forced motherhood upon me. He always saw Edie as his responsibility and insisted that I should just go about my life as normal and if I ever felt like doing some picking up of child or pulping of broccoli in my spare time

I was welcome to. For the most part I saw her as a mysterious little bundle he tended to in the bungalow every second day. I would watch her in Sime's arms and feel slightly overwhelmed. He had made a person. I made coffee.

Motherhood had always seemed an odd, unlikely future for me, on a par with suddenly waking up one morning and loudly announcing, 'I think I rather like the idea of being an amputee for a bit' and determinedly sawing off a leg. I had never shown a predilection for breeding the way Gabi had. When children were handed to me I went straight into consternation mode and held them awkwardly, stiffly, like a Lego attachment stuck on the wrong way. If they started crying there would be an instant sense of panic from both of us, me looking around desperately for adult assistance while the wracking sobs grew louder and more insistent and in need of proper grownup care. If none immediately arrived I would stuff the child under the couch til the crying grew mercifully silent. ('What's that strange muffled noise coming from the sofa?' 'Not sure. More wine?')

'Children sense fear,' Gabi would say, trying to coach me through the more difficult aspects of Holding a Child 101.

'What, like *dogs*?'

'Kind of. Like dogs with an inbuilt fire alarm.'

By three months into our relationship I was so outrageously in love Sime could have asked me to drink a mug of mucus each morning and I would have cheerily complied, so long as it was *his* mucus. He was a capable, warm, engaged parent and I envied the ease with which he interacted with his daughter. If he could do it, I wanted to learn. I imagined us pushing Edie on a swing, riding a horse on a beach, making a bed as a family and collapsing in fits of giggles beneath clean white linen. Those were my expectations of parenting. I had no point of reference outside of Kmart commercials and any film ever screened on the W channel between the hours of midday and 2 pm.

When he handed over baby and bottle I would stand there, arms and legs jutting out, like a halfwit coat-stand.

'But what do I *do* with her?' I would hiss at him.

He smiled.

'Just hold her.'

It was an impossible task, getting a grip on this squirming giblet, this molten lava. She was all softness and damp skin, cinnamon aromas. As I tried and tried again to wrangle her into the bath or hoist her screaming into a high chair, I could hear the continuous mantra pulsing through my head: *this child is not yours*.

I wanted to love her as my own but in those dark moments of frustration when I was helpless with rage and bewilderment, I was starkly reminded: she was somebody else's daughter and she was, for all intents and purposes, a stranger.

One day when Sime had pressing engagements at the Vic Markets he asked how I'd feel about spending a few hours alone with Edie while he went to work.

'Don't feel like you have to say yes,' he insisted. 'I can ask my mum.'

'Oh, come *on*,' I said with breezy assurance. 'We'll be *fine*. I *love* kids.'

He looked at me doubtfully. This was the same girl who had been left alone with his daughter at the Healesville Hotel for five minutes while he went to the toilet and announced with a perplexed frown upon his return, 'I think some vomit happened.'

Sime left more phone numbers with me than he knew people with phones, gave me a long hug for bravery along with a searching look which indicated he would come and hunt me down if anything bad happened to his child and he wouldn't be responsible for his actions, and then he closed the door behind him and I heard his car drive away.

Edie was in her high chair. She and I stared at each other for a long, wordless moment. One of us blew a gentle little snot bubble out of her nose, I can't recall who. Eventually I spoke.

'Well,' I said. 'I suppose we should start to get to know each other a little.'

It's difficult to get to know somebody who can't speak. I was used to showing off, trying to win people over with my collection of anecdotes and impressions. I held no faith in my personality without witty riposte, and children had a tendency to be unimpressed by an ability to wisecrack. Also I needed a straight man to work off. 'Hey, way to shit yourself' just doesn't cut it when the response is a blank gaze and small stream of drool, though obviously in the case of Nick 'The Wogboy' Giannopolous this sort of thing warrants a standing ovation.

A strange maternal instinct was supposed to kick in at this exact point. There was supposed to be a signal, or a whistle. Real women looked at babies and started instantaneously lactating. I was supposed to feel a yearning for baking pie. Instead I just wanted her to stop staring at me like Bride of Chucky.

When younger, I fancied myself as one day becoming one of those effortlessly cool mothers who spoke to their children as 'real people' and attempted to 'level' with them in times of high anxiety. 'Talk to me,' I imagined myself saying from an understanding crouching position as my offspring hit the deck wailing for a Bubble O' Bill. 'Let's workshop this out, one on one.' Of course this sort of logic flies out the window the first time a full-scale meltdown occurs and you find yourself singing 'INCY WINCY SPIDER' with the sort of brittle, shrill mania usually seen in Joan Crawford directly before she snaps a few coat hangers in half. Children will not suffer hypocrites or blowhards, a fact that strikes fear into the hearts of most of us who are, by nature, hypocrites or blowhards. A child's steady gaze is like X-Ray Specs into the black corners of your soul. There is nowhere to hide.

And that's when I inadvertently stumbled upon the same formula my folks had all those years before: draw on your theatre background. I put on a show. I threw myself into parenting like it was opening night for the Kew Amateur Players. I introduced costumes and wigs and changed the lyrics to well-known songs to include the names of our family. By the time Sime came home Edie and I were both in full pancake make-up and I was dressed as Little Orphan Annie.

'She likes me!' I said brightly. 'Look! She really likes me!'

After steering me gently from the room and removing the swimming cap from his daughter's head ('I think Daddy Warbucks might need a little rest, hon'), Sime had time to reflect upon my unique style of mothering. It may have been odd, it may have been rooted in that strange world of unhealthy, competitive mother-daughter showbusiness partnerships like Liza Minnelli and Judy Garland, or Matthew and Patti Newton, but it was my way of coming at what was a fairly challenging emotional situation and, given my upbringing, the only point of reference I had. Being raised by two actors ~~didn't fuck me up in the least~~ only affected me slightly and besides which Sime would be on hand to veto any of my more elaborate showpieces.

Awash with love, we decided to marry and make our strange little family unit official in the eyes of the baby Jesus, or at the very least create an excuse for excessive drinking in a rural environment. We joined together in a pine forest, me in a red nightgown and Sime in jeans and a trucker's cap. Our beloved Bubble of friends stood shivering in the cold, arms slung around each other, smiling indulgently at this grand, conventional gesture symbolising our mutual adoration. We felt young and handsome and impenetrable. Edie, nearly two years old, sat in a stroller during the ceremony, avocado smeared all over her perfect face, which is the best you can hope for with certain wedding guests. I carried her out of the forest, full of love and promise in my heart, and she pointed at me with a dirty finger. 'Mik,' she said with no small amount of pride. Sime and I looked at each other.

'She said your name.'

'Well, it wasn't *exactly* my name. She called me "Mik".'

The question had finally arisen about what Edie was going to call me when she was able to talk conversationally. I was now technically her stepmother, a title that sat on the scale of fairytale evil somewhere between a poisoned apple and Jeffrey Dahmer. I didn't want to be plain old 'Marieke'. There was no romanticism in that, no sense of family. I wanted to be someone special.

When as a teenager I had started calling my own mother by her Christian name—Galia—she became visibly upset.

'Anybody can call me *Galia*,' she said. 'You're the only person in the entire world who can call me Mum.'

I kept calling her Galia regardless because it seemed like the cooler thing to do and I was an insensitive adolescent out to hurt her feelings.

I was the only person in the world who Edie could call her stepmother. I wanted to make sure that what she called me was *right*. A friend's mother had insisted on being called 'Molly' by her new granddaughter and had spent months of babysitting coaching the infant.

'Who am I? I'm Molly. I'm *Molly*.'

When the girl was old enough to form the words, my friend's mother realised with a start that she'd essentially handed the opportunity to be called 'Grandma' over to someone else in the family. It had been a tactical error. Furiously, she tried to backpedal, creating a fusion of names the child could work with.

'Who am I? I'm GrandMol. *GrandMol.*'

It was to no avail. She was—and remains to this day, I believe—Molly. Grandma is on the other side of the family, no doubt immeasurably smug.

In the end we settled on 'Missus', which is what Sime called me when he wasn't cursing my very existence to the gods ho ho, and hearing Edie say it for the first time, with that clumsy, all-encompassing lisp almost every child struggles with at some point, was one of the most beautiful and life-affirming moments of my existence.

'Mithuth?'

She grew and she grew. It is what children do. Sime accepted my shortcomings as a parent and encouraged the blossoming petals of maternal instinct that were forcing their way through despite my best efforts to remain inept. I learned how to change a nappy while still holding a conversation, like Steve Martin in the final scene of *Parenthood*. I taught Edie the alphabet. I found that little nook 'twixt hip and shoulder where she balanced perfectly when I had other things to do, like get in and out of a car without causing a crowd of concerned citizens to gather around angrily, threatening to call DOCS.

Sime and I spent a happy week turning her room into an Arabian tent and presented it to her in song and dance. She learned all the words to 'Tomorrow' and *Pippin*'s 'Magic to

Do'. Soon I would start her in on *Godspell* and *42nd Street* and the circle of life would be complete. We shared custody, so spent half our time repeating the story of Maisy the Mouse in a dimly lit bedroom at one in the afternoon, and the other simply being young and hedonistic and madly in love. It was a delicate balance, and we got it right most of the time. Our friends knew which nights to call us out into wickedness, and which evenings we locked the doors and flourished as an unconventional family unit. We parented with and without hangovers. We parented with sweeping gestures and insignificant stumbles.

People thought Edie was mine and I didn't discourage them. It helped that she was so little and had those huge black eyes. When I ran into friends I hadn't seen in a while and I was holding an infant in my arms, I could see them do the *my god, I had no idea* face. I played a dangerous game, not confirming or denying either way. Enjoying the show-offy bit of motherhood, where your child is good-looking and everybody likes them.

'This is Edie. Say hello, Edie.'

'Hello.'

I would whisk her away before she could rumble the ruse by saying anything about me not being her real mother.

Our family was mismatched and extended. Edie would stay with my parents, Sime's parents, her mother's parents, her mother's sister. She adapted beautifully to this baffling rotisserie of houses and was a happy, well-adjusted child. I would take her to the park and lie in the grass with her and sing. Looking up at the clouds, our heads would touch.

In that moment, just the two of us and the sky, she was mine and I was hers.

We took baths together, the pair of us crammed into some ungodly garish tub while Sime made dinner, and happily wandered around naked in the bedroom afterwards. My family, too, had been a naked one. I would climb into bed with my parents of a morn and we'd all be naked as the day was long. When my dad levered himself from the mattress once, I heard myself gasp.

'Dad,' I said scandalously. 'You've got a stiffy.'

He sighed, and looked to my mother. She shrugged, one of those 'you're the one with the penis, you get this' moments.

My father sat down—carefully—on the bed.

'This, Marieke,' he said in a teacherly fashion, 'is what's rather crudely referred to as a "piss horn".' I nodded and took this in. Given their predilection for theatrics I suppose I'm lucky he didn't put on a puppet show with it.

In a naked moment I once bent down to get some clean underwear and noticed Edie had fallen silent. I turned to see her staring at me with an expression not far from awe.

'Gee,' she said quietly. 'You've got a really big bottom.'

I frowned.

'It's not *that* big.' Why was I arguing with a three-year-old?

She shook her head, refusing to accept my explanation.

'It's the *biggest bottom I've ever seen*,' she insisted, which was the point that I picked her up and threw her from the window.

When Edie was three-and-a-half her mother took her

on a two-week holiday to Brisbane and decided to stay. She wrote us a letter, explaining her case. 'I need to be near my family,' she said. 'This is too hard.'

We were both filled with an unbridled confusion. We were good parents, we put on shows and fed her vegetables and made her go to bed at a reasonable hour. And just like that, a cold war between two sad ex-lovers resulted in the loss of Edie from our little family unit.

There are, they say, hundreds of Inuit words for 'snow', and *x* amount of Latin words for 'love', but as far as I understand there is not one word in the known language that describes what it feels like for a once-reluctant stepmother to lose access to a child she has learned to raise.

It destroyed our relationship. Unable to fathom how such a gross miscarriage of justice could occur without some sensible authority figure stepping in to make things right, Sime and I fell apart. We kept Edie's room set up, as though she would return through the front door at any moment. We were like the parents of the dead. He had no bundle to cling to, nobody to sing to sleep. He tried to parent me and I railed against him. We should have gone to counselling. We didn't. We buried each other, and our relationship, into the ground.

I felt the loss of Edie keenly; mourned the child who had never been mine. It was a tangled grief. I did not know if I had the right to these feelings.

'It's not as though she was *your* kid,' somebody said to me. 'I mean, imagine how *Sime* must be feeling.'

A few years ago I was told by a doctor that I might never

have children of my own, at least not without the aid of drugs with complicated names or a vocal campaign by Deborra-Lee Furness. I accepted the news with an odd sort of calm. It felt like being told I would never fly. I wondered if my sole stab at mothering would involve those all-too-brief years with Sime and Edie. I regretted wrestling for so long with the concept itself. I regretted too few days at the park, looking up at the clouds, touching heads.

Edie's eleven now, and prefers to be called 'Bel', something I have trouble getting used to. I want to breathe into her hair and do zerberts on her bare belly but she doesn't like that anymore. Some years ago, she and her mother returned to Melbourne. I met her on a street, Sime holding her hand tightly, and for a moment we looked at each other. All the baths and musical theatre and bad op-shop clothing and hot chips on the bonnet of station wagons existed in the air between us in that split second. And then she broke free of Sime's grasp and belted forward to embrace me tightly around the waist.

'Missus!' she exclaimed. 'I've *missed* you!'

She still calls me Missus and still runs to hug me when we meet, all teeth and long hair and sticky-out arms. That she remains a part of my existence, in however an unorthodox fashion, is something I can never be grateful enough for. There may be other children in my life at some later stage; softly spoken products of a broken relationship whose refugee I am temporarily sheltering, but I understand now that I will never know that true ownership, the unspoken ritual of life-giving and innate selflessness. I was not born to be a mother but I have mothered, for a few blessed moments, a few precious hours, on a swing, in a bath, on a private stage made for two.

Parts of this story first appeared in Frankie *magazine.*

Man bites dog

Bob Ellis: a writer of no small reputation. A penner of political speeches, a Labor Party devotee, man of the theatre, filmmaker, author. Kim Beazley, the former leader of the ALP, once referred to Ellis, not entirely mean spiritedly, as 'Labor's pet cat'. The implication was that he held no real loyalty to the party, or to anybody really, was quite able to pen a speech singing the praises of Bob Carr whilst simultaneously shredding Julia Gillard on an ABC blog. Politicians from both sides would chuckle nervously on his approach, spotting from afar the lumbering, snarling man-camel shuffling his way down the corridors, taking long-suffering plods up the steps of Parliament House.

'Bob Ellis,' wrote columnist Frank Devine in *The Australian*, 'is more poisonous than a funnel web spider.'

The editor of the *Adelaide Review*, Christopher Pearson, was even less kind.

'Ellis' behaviour is often infantile . . . he has got into the habit of believing that he'll be endlessly indulged and forgiven because he's a wordsmith and because he's a larger-than-life, larger-than-lunch character.'

Bob Ellis was slovenly, to put it mildly. He was overweight, his pants slouched moodily below his belly. His thinning hair was painstakingly combed to one side. He was famously covered in stains and gave off a curious aroma of caffeine and sweat and anxiety. 'He used to be quite the ladies' man,' I was told on several occasions, usually by women who would punctuate the articulation with a dainty little shudder, to indicate that those days were well and truly over and they would have no trouble saying no were Ellis to ever come knocking at their door.

Yet photographs existed of him in his university years, a rake with mischievous eyes and sensual lips and there were even now moments, during a pointed wink or a glance upwards from a tightly gripped lectern, when that roué could be glimpsed again.

His writing was a sermon from the mount, delivered in a perfumed envelope flecked with spittle. Just take this 80th birthday message to Rupert Murdoch for a moment:

> His pink-cheeked lapdog (David) Cameron has already lost 2014 by tripling university fees. And then he will be 83, with nowhere to go. And his mother will be 108 and still think him a shallow, bumptious disappointment to the memory of his father Keith, exposer of Gallipoli . . . He deserves no less. The Iraq adventure, which was to a great extent his project, has killed tens of thousands of children and driven into miserable

exile millions of useful middle-class people including almost all of Iraq's dentists, levelled Babylon and looted or burned its glorious museums and libraries, irreplaceable now and ended the education of its women . . .

And he has done much to hobble the English language, making all political statement a corseted, evasive half-truth and most politicians (like Gillard) blitherers of cliché.

He deserves, at 80, his fate. Happy birthday, Rupert. May you sleep uneasily, my dread dark lord, tonight.

Parry, thrust, STAB STAB STAB MAIM, delicate skip, sob: that was the inestimably devastating prose of Ellis.

Given the venom in that brilliant pen of his there were bound to be detractors, and there were, there still are, hundreds of them, thousands. Ellis never failed to give them new fodder with which to undermine him. He slandered at will, found himself in a farcical legal stoush with conservative bullyboys Tony Abbott and Peter Costello (for daring to suggest that Costello's god-fearing wife, Tanya, had ever behaved in a fashion that was less than saintly), and inspired the loyal readers of the women's glossies into a chorus of condemnation and distasteful nose-wrinkling when he knocked up a screenwriter, apparently behind some flapping canvas marquee at a writers' festival. Matters were hardly improved when, in a misguided sense of defence, he claimed to be incapable of an erection. 'Penetration was briefly achieved . . . before a not unprecedented bout of impotence . . . concluded by oral sex,' he read in a statement on radio station 2BL, causing a nation to as one murmur 'TMI' and attempt gamely to swallow the rising vomit in their throats.

And yet there was something in his writing that knocked me down like a prizefighter. There were certain passages in *Goodbye Jerusalem* that made me weep, or gulp frantically for air as though drowning. His words would seethe and spark, burning across the page like scrub fire. Sometimes I would have to close his books and rest my head on their covers, overwhelmed. I feared that if I read further the pages would come alive like *The Neverending Story* and I would find myself riding a luckdragon named Falkor through the skies of Canberra.

Bob Ellis was punk, a simmering pot of vitriol who couldn't give a fuck about the opinions of others and felt so violently revolted by the state of Australian politics that he simply shoved aside convention and manners to say what desperately needed to be said. He cared not for the delicacies of libel laws, nor correct legal procedure. In mixed gatherings he would have no hesitation in referring to unsubstantiated rumour about the sexual predilections of certain Liberal politicians as though it was plain fact, as though he'd personally walked into a hotel room and found them in the act of having sex with a sheep or meddling with a child, and hurried out again with pardons and gasps. Occasionally he spoke the truth. Often he just said the first thing that came into his head, and backed it up with a great wash of feeling. Those who knew him well took his venting diatribes with a grain of salt. I devoured every word. He was a necessary raw wound on an otherwise sanitised Australian political landscape.

My obsession knew no bounds. In 2000 I became the owner of a perfect Staffordshire Bull-Terrier, six weeks old and caramel with a white neckerchief patch on her chest. I was instantly besotted, following her around the house with the devotion of a new parent.

I named her Bob Ellis.

'To hell with gender rules!' I said, to anybody who would listen. 'She is a she, and Bob Ellis the man is a he, and they exist in separate realms. Allow me my starry-eyed folly.'

When I told my usually very open-minded and left-wing friend Ben I had named my dog Bob Ellis, his face had twisted into a mask of venom.

'Why?' he sneered. 'Is your dog a cunt?'

This sort of thing would happen regularly when I took Bob Ellis to the park, or out walking. Strangers would approach with smiles, squatting down and murmuring hellos and asking requisite dog-owner questions about how old she was and wasn't she lovely and how did I get her darling little coat so soft. Some of them, after asking her name, would look up at me sharply with no small amount of horror and disgust.

'Bob *Ellis*?' asked one very dear older lady.

I nodded.

'Why would you . . . how could you do such a terrible thing to this sweet, sweet dog?'

She was backing off now, shaking her head, as though even being in our immediate vicinity would taint her with the bacteria of evil and cause her to burst into sudden flame. 'Bob Ellis?? That's just . . . that's just cruel, that's nothing short of *cruel*.'

She was in tears when she finally walked away.

Sometimes I would try to cut this sort of confrontation off at the pass, to avoid the conflict, run the words together as though I had invented an eccentric little faerie name for my dog.

'What's she called?' a smiling man would ask.

'Bobellis,' I would reply. The intonation would change, favouring incomprehension. *Bah*bells. Bobbles. Boppellesse. It was a safe name to use around children as they didn't know any better and hadn't yet formed an opinion on Bob's writing or politics.

'I love Bob Ellis!' I would hear a friend's three-year-old say to his mother and I would feel immense satisfaction. This is how we work on the left side of politics. We indoctrinate children and brainwash them with music and puppies.

In 2004 the devotion was taken a step further, and I had inked on my right arm a combined homage to Ellis and Kurt Vonnegut. 'And so on, and so it goes' it reads, winding around a pair of oriental lilies, a walking billboard for the impetuousness of the young and the passion of one particularly besotted twenty-eight-year-old girl. In heated discussions I made excuses for Bob's at times archaic statements regarding women and abortion.

'He grew up in a religious fundamentalist family,' I would say shrilly to naysayers. 'It's not as if he has a *choice*.'

My grandfather had died in 1994, suffering an almighty lightning strike of a heart attack whilst reading the form guide. He had been a left-wing author, brilliant, cantankerous, womanising, tortured, and so admired for his storytelling skills he would sit in pubs for hours, preferring to regale a room full of strangers with anecdotes than go home to some long-suffering and temporary girlfriend.

'Did I ever tell you the yarn about the gunslinger from Gunnedah?' he would start, packing tobacco into his pipe, and feeling in his brimming coat pocket for notes of his story.

Frank's life was chaotic and acerbic. He was once arrested for a swathe of unpaid parking fines, and ran for parliament twice, unsuccessfully. He despised authority and even after leaving the Communist Party carried the acidity of a rebel. When his daughter married a policeman he would make it a habit to call the house at two in the morning, drunk, railing at the piss-disgraceful corruption in the force. My aunt and uncle learned that in such a frame of mind Frank was not to be argued with, and would simply put the phone receiver under the bed until he shouted himself out. Some nights they could just hear him still, a tinny little enflamed warble under the doona, an impassioned plea for sanity no bigger than a pea beneath the mattress of a princess.

Ellis and Frank shared many similar qualities and with no grandparents remaining alive I found myself subconsciously gravitating towards Bob at Writers Guild events or screen conferences. I met him for the first time at Sydney Wharf, an auspicious occasion I am almost certain he doesn't remember, and approached with heart and cheeks aflame.

'Mr Ellis—I'm Frank's granddaughter,' I began, hoping that the inroad of family would assuage any fears he may have when he later discovered I had a dog at home sharing his name and a huge spray of ink on my right shoulder in part inspired by his work.

'Your grandfather was a brilliant man,' Bob opined sweepingly. 'Brilliant. We spent a great deal of time together. We were going to stage a play chronicling the life of Ben Chifley . . .'

It kept going, a stream of important pontifications and meanderings. He would talk as though delivering a lecture at a state dinner. I ended the afternoon curled at his feet, transfixed, like a particularly attentive pouffe he might have absentmindedly stretched out and rested his feet on at any moment. After a time he seemed to forget I was there and just kept telling stories into mid-air, holding court to an empty foyer. Ellis didn't need an audience, and I was too awestruck to interrupt or ask questions. We fit together very well.

Ellis and I skirted around each other for some years after that. I would spot him from afar at opening nights, or pacing the foyer of the ABC looking furious about some perceived slight on behalf of the national broadcaster. A boyfriend and I went to see him launch a book at Readings and stood out the front like teenagers waiting to meet Roxette. When Bob approached we fell apart with mortified giggles and stammers.

'We have a dog . . . my dog . . . she's in the car,' I gestured with annoyingly trembling fingers.

'I love dogs,' replied Ellis shortly, apparently not knowing or caring who we were, nor wishing to wait around and get to know two blushing fuckwits pointing inanely out onto the street. He nodded politely and ambled away. My boyfriend and I looked at each other and, after a pause, squealed delightedly. I was hopping up and down on the spot. Bob Ellis was my Justin Bieber.

We met again at the 2020 summit and this time he seemed to remember me. We exchanged numbers—I apparently had some legitimacy now, working as an opinion writer—and in time began occasionally texting, on election nights or during some political scandal I had worked myself into a froth over. In time he invited my partner and I to come and stay with him and his family for the weekend.

'Ellis is my hero,' I fretted to Tim beforehand. 'Should you really spend the weekend with your hero? Shouldn't you just stalk them at the AFI awards and leave creepy anonymous messages on their website instead?'

Heroes are just that because they are elusive, mute, flawless. We admire them from a distance and Blu-Tak their pictures to our wall without ever having to see them stumble down drunk or, in the case of stumbling down drunks, sober and doing yoga. We don't humanise them because they are not, in our eyes, human. We certainly shouldn't go and stay with them for a weekend.

But we did accept the offer.

Bob had given us messy, complicated instructions to get to his house and told us to call or text when we were close so he could meet us on the road.

'Our driveway is very easy to miss,' he said with sighs, as though the degenerate council had deliberately planned it thus.

We drove out of inner Sydney and up to Palm Beach. It was a warm day and we had the windows of our van rolled down. Tim played bootleg copies of the Bob Dylan Theme Time Radio Hour, loud. We were up to 'Coffee'. Dylan's voice flatlined through the car.

'Imagine we were going to spend the night at Dylan's house,' Tim said.

'He's a grumpy old cow too, apparently.'

'Or Tom Waits! We could go and stay in his junkyard palace.'

Palm Beach was as idyllic as Ellis had described, strolling couples with very white teeth laughing in a carefree fashion as they passed by sprawling cafes. Everything seemed clean and rich.

We rounded a sharp corner and saw him standing there, shirt untucked, belly protruding, a hulking figure, one of Satan's lollipop ladies. He pointed to a scooped-out section of cliffside and told us to park there, in front of his ancient Volvo. It was difficult to negotiate, particularly on a hair-pin bend with oncoming traffic tooting with irritation, and almost immediately Tim started to panic.

'I can't reverse park while Bob Ellis is watching me!' he whispered.

We could see Bob pointing and directing and flapping his arms around and saying something loud we couldn't quite figure out, or at least not until we heard our van hit Bob's car with a sickening crack.

'Oh,' said Tim. 'I guess he meant for us to stop.'

Bob looked disgusted when we emerged from the car full of apologies, and waved an angry hand in our direction as though he didn't want to hear it.

'It's just a fucking scratch,' he said, with a face like thunder.

The house itself was set atop a cliff, a soaring Vesuvius. We had expected a winding, crumbling staircase, cut into the earth, bracketed by a wooden barrier. It was difficult to understand why Bob was still so fat given that he had to climb Mount Everest every day.

Bob pointed again.

'Get in,' he said.

It was a small, roofless cage, about waist high, big enough for three or four children to play inside comfortably. We looked to Bob for further instructions, helpless tourists.

'It's a fucking inclinator!' he snapped, losing patience. 'And it takes us up to the house. Now get *in*.'

Tim picked up Bob Ellis the dog and we obediently stepped into the cage. Bob squeezed his considerable frame in front of us, causing an already uncomfortable arrangement to become borderline unbearable. We were like the cast of *The Magic Roundabout* stuck in a wheelie bin. Bob pressed a button and we jolted forward aggressively. The impact was such that I flew backwards and accidentally pressed the emergency stop lever. We shuddered to an immediate halt.

'What happened?' said Bob.

I felt his temper rising. I gestured wordlessly at the controls.

Bob started up the machine again. Again, I was flung back and managed to inadvertently bring everything to a stop.

Ellis was apoplectic. At this point it looked as though we would all die here, in this inclinator, sadly stuck down the bottom of a hill. Tim had his face buried in the dog's fur.

'When I push this button,' Bob explained, as though speaking to a pair of deaf children, 'we will move forward. If you are able to . . . *try not to turn the fucking thing off again.*'

The inclinator itself, when it got going, moved at a pace best described as 'leisurely'. We were essentially in a motorised wheelchair on an angle. Two men, a dog, and a chastened superfan. When we finally reached the summit—thank christ, thank christ—Bob Ellis the dog leaped from Tim's arms, impatient to explore. We watched her fondly and mutely for a moment as she sniffed the grass. Which did then seem an opportune moment for her to splay her back legs out and propel herself across Bob's lawn, rubbing her itchy backside with what appeared to be an enormous amount of care.

This went on for a very long time. Bob Ellis the man watching Bob Ellis the dog cheerily wiping her rectum all over his otherwise impeccable lawn.

Bob turned to us. He looked angry. To be fair, he always

looked angry. But at this point he looked slightly angrier than normal.

'Is your dog a *fool*?' he asked with relish, not waiting to hear the answer, just stomping indoors and announcing to his wife that the guests were here, was the kettle on and could we all just have a nice cup of tea.

Tim whispered urgently for Bob Ellis the dog to perhaps abandon her ablutions and act normal, or something along those lines. She trotted over obediently, tail wagging, looking up at us to see what fun we had to offer.

As we stood together, wondering what other ways we could fuck up this weekend, we looked out at the vista. It was a startlingly gorgeous view. Glimmering water, distant green islands. The hum of speedboats being commandeered by their playboy owners drizzled upwards. Foliage sighed in that thick, erotic, coastal way. It felt as though we looked down on all the world, and all the world was a sunny playground for the well-heeled set.

'Probably the best view in the country,' Ellis said importantly, reappearing by our sides, not looking at it, just squinting at us to ascertain our reactions. I felt sick with anxiety, not wanting to say the wrong thing. We had already dented his car and broken his inclinator. Then our dog had run her anus all over his lawn.

Bob's thundery rages were of biblical proportions. I wasn't sure I would cope if he suddenly unleashed one on me.

We ate well, a vegetable curry and poppadoms and rice, everybody politely murmuring over the fact that Annie had gone out of her way to make vegan food. Ellis was distracted, or seemed to be, and ate in great gulps, shovelling curry into his mouth. He spilled raita across the table.

'You can rest after lunch,' he said. 'And later we'll go to the movies.'

Everything had a surreal edge. I was unable to relax, wanting to say something so impressive and astute that Bob would look up from his food with admiring eyes. It was impossible to get a word in most of the time, so we mostly sat and listened.

Bob and Annie's daughter, Jenny, we were told, was elsewhere in the house, mourning the recent death of a friend. 'You probably won't see her,' Annie whispered to us, but I did, running into her later that afternoon in the kitchen. Jenny and I were the same age. She looked at me with open curiosity as the dog sat at my feet.

'So this,' she said slowly, 'is Bob Ellis the dog.'

I imagined what this moment must feel like from her perspective. I pictured waking up in my own parents' house and walking into another room to find a young woman standing and grinning at me in a friendly yet demented fashion.

'This is my dog, Alan Hardy!!' she would exclaim with enthusiasm, before rolling up her sleeve to show me the tattoo she had designed inspired by my father's myriad acting roles.

Jenny and I stared at each other. I have rarely felt so foolish.

'Well,' I said with forced cheer. 'Better go see what Tim's up to.'

Bob insisted we go to the local cinema to see *Vicky Cristina Barcelona*. He was seeing it for the ninth time. 'It's a work of genius,' he kept repeating, 'complete genius. Woody Allen is back in form.' I loved this about Bob; that he would enjoy something so much he wanted to share it with everybody he met, even strangers. Three years later he would take me to see *The Wharf Revue*. It would be my first visit and his fourteenth.

During the film, Bob cackled and sighed, muttered admiringly, and heckled. He kept looking over to us, ensuring that we were gaining as much enjoyment from it as he was, that we too were appreciating the nuances and craftsmanship. After the film we went for dinner at the local Chinese, and Ellis held court over the Lazy Susan, spilling wine and sweet and sour sauce across the paper tablecloth as he reiterated exactly why the movie worked and why we should be duly awed and why Julia Gillard was a cunt. We had gelato after the meal and strolled the deserted Palm Beach promenade. An empty Burger Rings packet danced past our feet and flung itself in a suicide mission against a rock. Ellis was too drunk to drive so Tim commandeered the Volvo back to the house.

That night we sat for hours, eating liqueur chocolates liqueurs and drinking port and listening to Bob rail about the state of the New South Wales Labor party, John Howard, the sorry demise of Kim Beazley. Pet subjects, and we had heard most of them before, but we sat and soaked it up anyway. It was like a free concert. Ellistock.

Tim eventually announced he was going to bed. It was 2 am. Bob reached for the port again. I wanted to stay and hear more, to have some one-on-one time with that wonderful mind. Tim nudged me.

'You're probably tired too,' he said meaningfully.

Those knowing looks other women had given me when I proclaimed my devotion to Bob suddenly came sharply into focus. If Bob made a pass at me when we were alone I would have fallen apart. This was not how I saw his role in my life. I wanted to give him space and stay out of his way, just so he wouldn't be tempted in the first place. This was not a sexual relationship. This was an exchange of ideas.

In bed, I whispered with Tim.

'He wouldn't have *done* anything. He was too pissed.'

'You don't know that for sure. I saw him trying to look down your dress.'

'He was probably just drunk and cross-eyed. He's not like that anymore. He's not like that with *me*.'

There had always been, I suppose, the question of sex.

'Are you going to fuck him?' somebody had asked me once.

'What, *Ellis*? Are you out of your mind?'

'He might expect it.'

'Don't be revolting.'

'He does have an eye for the ladies, you know. And there you are, all young and juicy and adoring . . .'

'It's not that kind of thing. Besides which, Ellis is past his philandering days. He said so in that letter he read out on the radio about not being able to get it up anymore.'

On my part, at least, the relationship was entirely innocent.

I was in it purely for his cerebral cortex. The way Bob wrote split me open and connected to something valuable, something I had never possessed yet felt like I had lost. The older man/younger woman dynamic didn't titillate or interest me at all. If anything, it felt as though my sex got in the way of an average, healthy, garden-variety hero worship. If I were a young man, I told myself, nobody would care that I had Bob's picture up on my studio wall and would talk to it in the mornings before starting work.

The next day we took the dog for a stroll on the beach—Bob seemed to have forgiven her rather forward introduction of the previous afternoon—and went out for breakfast, where he spilled egg and coffee across the table and himself.

We said relieved goodbyes and made a vague date to go and see a movie in a few weeks' time. In retrospect, the ensuing mix-up was entirely generational—I had said yes, presuming that we would confirm closer to the date.

It was still difficult to quell that frisson I felt when receiving texts from Ellis. There he was, a name in my phone, right between Blue and Booky.

Oh, just a text from Bob Ellis, I would tell people casually. *I think we're going to the movies together.*

Friends had enjoyed a brief period of cracking wise when I first got the hound—I didn't know your dog could text, etcetera. I had allowed them their levity. There was something about receiving a text or an email from someone you admired. For a brief moment you were catapulted up into their peer group, conversing with the gods. I had felt this way when I was introduced to Patti Smith backstage at the Big Day Out.

'How are you?' she had asked, politely.

'Food,' I replied, having clearly been confused as to whether I had wanted to say 'fine' or 'good' and settling instead for an interesting combination of the two. Patti Smith had walked away. The gods had closed the door.

The next I heard of our movie date was when Ellis called me. He was standing in front of the cinema, he said, and had travelled all the way from Palm Beach for the occasion we had specifically agreed on. Where the fuck was I?

Everything froze.

'I thought you were going to text and confirm,' I said feebly.

He hung up. He was furious.

'Bob Ellis just hung up on me,' I told my friend Lindsay.

'I didn't know your dog could use the phone,' said Lindsay, tediously.

Man and dog became so commonplace people stopped making jokes. Bob Ellis was my dog, who I loved more than life itself. Bob Ellis was a writer. They were simply now two unconnected things that shared the same name.

Bob and I didn't see each other for a while after that, me tentatively keeping my distance as he cursed me as a flighty youth to anybody who would listen. A gentle peace was eventually reached and yet months later when I was unable to help him launch his book he was almost apoplectic with rage all over again. 'I suppose I shall have to ask Tony Abbott instead,' he bellowed, and he did. The book was launched roughly twenty-four hours after Abbott had taken over the Liberal leadership and the eyes of the nation were trained upon Gleebooks. In hindsight I had done Bob a favour.

I insisted on his being on the bill at the inaugural Men of Letters event I was co-organising, amongst more commercially well-known types like Matt Preston and Tim Rogers and Eddie Perfect. He was obviously uncomfortable, pacing in the foyer before the show, complaining about sharing the stage with 'fucking comedians'. I sent Gabi to placate him, but he was growing tetchy and impossible. He insisted he wanted to leave, he should never have come. Gabi returned to me with a worried look.

'I got him a glass of red,' she said. 'But he seems fairly pissed off.'

'He's always pissed off,' I told her. 'That's why he's a genius.'

When it came time for him to speak he lumbered to the lectern, took a breath, and within moments had silenced the room. He spoke, from the heart, of his wife. He spoke of their many miscarriages, the trials and tribulations of their marriage, his mistakes, his regrets. It was a piece rubbed raw with honesty, and Bob delivered it in the patented 'cadence of the King James Bible' that David Marr had once admiringly fashioned as his oratory signature.

He received a standing ovation. Everybody wept.

This, I thought to myself. *This is why*.

I felt like my hoarse devotion of Ellis had culminated in that moment. I actually went around to various people at the event saying, 'See? See?' I wanted to sing him from the rooftops.

He knew he had done well and looked like a prince backstage afterwards, accepting congratulations, beaming delightedly and passing opinion on everyone and everything in the room. When he saw me he swept me up in a big sweaty toxic embrace. All was forgiven. His eyes were glistening with proud tears.

'That was brilliant, Bob. Thank you.'

He leaned into my ear.

'If that's not worth a blowjob,' he whispered. 'Nothing is.'

Our relationship seemed to level out after that. Perhaps now that sex had made its ugly presence felt it created the necessity of distance. He would send me a text once every few months, or I would see him at a book launch, and I would hug him and nod and smile and listen to his latest spray on Kevin Rudd. And then I would go home and read his novels and diaries and his articles on the ABC website and I would seamlessly re-enter that world of infatuation where he remained infallible, he remained distant, and would never, ever suffer the indignity of being human.

• • •

TO MARIEKE, FOR HER MEMOIR

I'd had some trouble with a younger single female in recent years. She kept me waiting for nine hundred and twenty-seven days for the return of the sex we began with, and came late, or didn't turn up to, a hundred of the writing sessions—in Adelaide, the Adelaide Hills, Melbourne and Sydney—of a film based on her life called *Honeymoon Girl* and didn't turn up to meet the producers, actors and funding bodies either.

So when I learned, six years after the event, that Marieke Hardy had named her dog after me, after I had met her and she had said, 'You write like Hemingway,' at the 2020, I was attracted to her chest and her intellect—in that order—but feared she'd be like the previous one, a glittering tease.

And when I drove from Gosford to see *Hunger* with her, grope her and force her down on my dick and SHE DIDN'T TURN UP and couldn't be reached on her mobile, this seemed to be true. Her excuse, that I hadn't confirmed it, was either valid or not, but I was very angry, not just because of my geographical inconvenience but because she was, or seemed, exactly like Tracey Rohrsheim in all aspects including beauty, wit and insanity, and I wrote her off.

Things changed a bit with her texts of apology and her continuing public utterance of her adoration of me.

She broke up with her bloke and bought me a superb meal she paid for in three figures, but there were three panes of clear glass between us and it was clear no sex would occur though she was famous for spreading it around, like Jacki Weaver when young, with good humour and great intelligence.

I decided to leave her alone, in every sense. I did this three or four times. Then I thought she might be helpful in getting me on television and kept in touch with her. I gave her a book she hadn't read, and a play she still hasn't read, and a series pilot with a role for her in it she hasn't read either.

What is a coquette?

Well, like Audrey Hepburn, a similar girl with a smaller chest, in *Breakfast at Tiffany's*. What one character calls a *real* phoney.

It would be different if we lived in the same town. We'd be meeting regularly on Monday nights and reading out paragraphs of great books to each other.

But geography, old age, fatness and (yes) intermittent impotence has intervened.

Disappointed? Oh yes. Still keen? Less so. Think she's gorgeous? Yes. And brilliant? Absolutely.

And so it goes . . .

An afterword by my ex-boyfriend Tim

When I first went to her place, she sat me down with a premixed can of gin and tonic and pulled out a book by Ivan Brunetti—the graphic artist. She said, 'I like how beautiful this is . . . he writes about suicide the whole time.' I looked up at her. How strange it seemed to me to find these things beautiful. Where I was from suicide was sad, dark and troubled, not really associated with beautiful. But this small woman, with deep brown eyes and a cluttered flat that looked like Sherlock Holmes's place mixed with the British Museum, was pulling me into a strange sort of fix.

We fell in love not long after, propelled by a shared interest in the people who railed against and defied the mundane. Writers like Bukowski and Fante, Flannery O'Connor and John Cheever. The ones who write about the sad, the bad, the mad. I certainly was exposed to many things I normally would have missed if not for her—and, I hope, vice versa. We travelled together, lived together, moved houses together, moved interstate together, all for a long while. She is one of my best friends.

We had a sometimes difficult relationship, two personalities that clashed, but I don't want to talk about that here—that is for us. And, though the harder moments were hard, we both knew we had found something very special together and the sweet times will be with me always.

In any relationship, you see people very closely and I had been witness to a lot of her trouble, but the task of writing a book was something I strongly kept urging her to do. And so, stories started taking shape and some were finished, which was wonderful. When talking about this book she was to write, she kept telling me she wanted to write about the truth and the 'hard' things—again, something we both admired in others' work.

Some things you can only do alone, I guess, and there are secrets inside her, still hidden from me. I have tried to learn not to shy away from her because of that; she has told me so many secrets already.

Late last year, we broke up. It was complicated and tiring—mostly achingly frustrating. I had to go and find someplace else to live. I was through with the thought of perpetual and confused heartbreak. I had to try and move on. Which involved a lot of drinking and it was a sad time. It still is some days.

To see myself in print feels like I'm a 'character', and that's a strange feeling. Going to Bob Ellis's home was hilarious, probably because we were both a bit nervous. I was in hysterics for the most part. I find the prostitute story very funny too, and I admire the strength of truth in her words.

The potential reaction from friends and family to some stories makes me feel uneasy sometimes, probably because I don't want them to misjudge her. To be brutally honest and frank takes a lot of balls and it's very easy for other people to sit safely on the other side and judge. But it'll be okay. It always is, somehow.

The darkness, I've learnt—after that first time at her joint with Brunetti—is as present as the light, and the mundane and 'normal' get too much attention. Some things won't go away and they should be celebrated.

Thank you, darling Marieke.

Acknowledgements

Heartfelt thankyous:

Tim, Gabi, Gen, Mitch, Sugar, Fluffy, Booky, Hotman, Slam, Luscy, Sime, Bel, Alice, The Conti, Michaela McGuire, Lee Sandwith, Benjamin Law, Lorelei Vashti, Kirsty Fisher, Dan Kelly, Larky, Claire Collins, Women of Letters, Lindsay McDougall, Edgar's Mission, Ben Ball, Ronnie Scott, First Tuesday Book Club, The Bubble, Jo Lyons, Jane Palfreyman, d.a. calf, The Book Grocer, and a dog named Bob Ellis.

Oh, and Mum and Dad . . . if we're still on speaking terms. x